Caring about animals is not enough — we need to take *action* to reduce suffering and save animal lives. This is the book that gives you the information you need so *you* can make a difference.

Some incredible facts from *The Animal Rights Handbook...*

*Only 10% of the American population hunts. But did you know that *your* tax dollars subsidize agencies that administer hunting programs?

*Sometimes, one person can make a big difference. After Berke Breathed criticized the Mary Kay cosmetics company in his "Bloom County" comic strip, the company stopped animal testing. Find out which companies are making efforts to prevent animal suffering.

*For every "target" animal trapped by fur trappers, two "non-target" animals are caught and killed. Trappers call these animals — such as dogs, cats, and deer — "trash animals."

*There are now over 15 million vegetarians in the U.S. — and the number has nearly doubled in the last decade.

THE ANIMAL RIGHTS HANDBOOK
Everyday Ways to Save Animal Lives

THE ANIMAL RIGHTS HANDBOOK

Everyday Ways
to Save Animal Lives

BERKLEY BOOKS, NEW YORK

The information contained in this book has been obtained primarily from publicly available sources, rather than from private sources or independent research not otherwise available to the public. However, we can't and don't guarantee the accuracy of all the information. This book offers you a start. The responsibility for using it ultimately rests with you.

THE ANIMAL RIGHTS HANDBOOK

A Berkley Book / published by arrangement with
Living Planet Press

PRINTING HISTORY
Berkley edition / February 1993

All rights reserved.
Copyright © 1990 by Living Planet Press.
Writing and research: Laura Fraser, Stephen Zawistowski,
Joshua Horwitz, Stephen Tukel.
Inside illustrations: Debbie Drechsler.
This book may not be reproduced in whole or in part,
by mimeograph or any other means, without permission.
For information address: The Berkley Publishing Group,
200 Madison Avenue, New York, New York 10016.

ISBN: 0-425-13762-7

A BERKLEY BOOK ® TM 757,375
Berkley Books are published by The Berkley Publishing Group,
200 Madison Avenue, New York, New York 10016.
The name "BERKLEY" and the "B" logo
are trademarks belonging to Berkley Publishing Corporation.

PRINTED IN THE UNITED STATES OF AMERICA

10 9 8 7 6 5 4 3 2 1

CONTENTS

*Our task must be to free ourselves . . .
by widening our circle of compassion to
embrace all living creatures and the
whole of nature and its beauty.*

—Albert Einstein

FOREWORD

This book just made my life a lot easier.

Every year I talk to thousands of people about animal rights—in every imaginable setting, including school assemblies, community meetings, on the phone, and in my office at the ASPCA. As a former college teacher, there is nothing I enjoy more than the spirited exchange of ideas and information.

But these discussions often conclude with a fresh barrage of questions. "Where can I get more information on cruelty-free products?" "What can I read to learn the facts about the fur industry?" "How can I do more to help stop product testing on animals?"

Until now, finding comprehensive animal rights information has been a daunting task. To answer even the simplest question I would have to steer the curious to a pamphlet from one animal rights group, to a brochure from a second group, and to a magazine from still a third. Answering more complex questions usually required exhaustive research that could discourage the most ardent inquirer.

More than once I said to myself: "Wouldn't it be great if there were one book . . ."

And now there is.

You're holding in your hands the single most effective weapon in the struggle for animal rights—*information*. For the very first time, everything you need to know about fur ranching, product testing, factory farming, and many other animal rights issues has been culled from hundreds of different sources and organized into a single, highly readable volume. And that is no small feat.

Yet this book is more than a compendium of important information. It's *useable* information.

It's one thing to learn that animals suffer unnecessarily in product testing. It's quite another to know how to use your consumer buying power to combat it. The cruelty of factory farming may not be news to you, but do you know how and where to find meat and dairy products that are not derived from cruel animal husbandry practices?

Now any concerned individual has the power to immediately diminish animal exploitation and abuse. You don't have to carry a placard or even write a letter to be an animal rights activist (though if you want to speak out, Chapter Seven will tell you how). Your consumer buying power is as potent as any other person's. And that power counts.

This book comes not a moment too soon. The number of people committed to animal rights is growing every day. It is a broad movement—as diverse as our nation's populace. While there may be disagreement among us concerning objectives and strategies, we all share a deeply held belief in the need for human and nonhuman animals to live in harmony.

The Animal Rights Handbook is a book that will unite, not divide. It brings us back to the abiding principle of animal rights: that nonhuman animals deserve to live according to their own natures, free from harm and abuse. It invites each and every one of us in our daily lives to courageously and consistently walk the path of respect and compassion for all living things.

—John F. Kullberg, Ed.D.
President
The American Society for the
Prevention of Cruelty to Animals

THE ANIMAL RIGHTS HANDBOOK

SHARING THE PLANET
WITH ANIMALS

SHARING THE PLANET
WITH ANIMALS

There is a moment in each of our lives when our heart first reaches out to an animal.

Perhaps it's a moment of wonder at the beauty and grace of a wild animal, or a feeling of compassion for a helpless creature in distress. Or maybe it's an instant of direct emotional connection with a cat or dog or horse. In that moment, the wall separating humans from other animal species melts away. From then on, we feel a kinship with the animals who share our planet.

In that same moment, something else begins to grow within us. We gradually become aware of how systematically most human beings exploit animals for their own gain. We begin to see that animal cruelty is deeply embedded in our society—in the way we eat and dress, in the products we use, and even in the ways we choose to entertain ourselves.

How we respond to this dawning awareness of animal suffering is one true measure of our humanity.

The most common response is denial. Animal cruelty seems too interwoven into the fabric of society—and into our own lifestyle—to be undone. No one person can make a difference, we think. It's easier to get on with life and worry about other problems.

And yet, once we glimpse the depth and breadth of animal suffering, it's often impossible to resume life where we left off. That's when the second, more challenging path presents itself: the path of compassionate living.

Compassionate living isn't very hard. But it does take a

commitment to change, and to action—beginning with small actions.

First, we have to reexamine our assumptions about how we treat animals in our daily lives. Can we love a cat or dog but eat other animals for dinner? Is an exotic wild animal more deserving of protection than a cow? Or, for that matter, a mouse? What are we teaching our children about our relation to animals when we take them to zoos or to the circus?

The next step on the path to compassionate living is self-education. We need to learn how farm animals are raised and how animals suffer needlessly for new product testing. We have to ask hard questions about what goes on in animal research laboratories and whether our government is using our tax dollars to hurt or help animals.

Finally, we must act. Because animal suffering will not abate until each of us takes responsibility for the choices we make in our daily lives. Each of us, as a consumer, has a profound impact on the fate of animals.

When you decide, for instance, to buy a cotton jacket instead of a fur-trimmed coat, you are sending an unmistakable message to clothes manufacturers: "Cotton jackets will earn you a profit. Killing animals for their fur will lose you money—and earn you only shame." Every time we enter a supermarket or drug store or department store, we are faced with cruel and compassionate alternatives. And the consumer choices you and I make *directly* affect animal lives.

More and more people have begun to make a commitment to compassionate living. The form that commitment takes varies from person to person. Some people stop eating meat; others exclude all animal products from their diet. One person may decide not to buy a fur coat, while another might also stop wearing leather. But every individual act of compassion makes a difference. Choosing to act consciously and compassionately, in ways large or small, is an essential principle underlying animal rights.

The planet we inhabit belongs to all living things. Every

species contributes something special to the Earth's miraculous diversity and beauty. Defending the rights of all animals to a life free from exploitation and abuse is one of the greatest contributions we humans can make.

HOW TO USE THIS BOOK

A belief in the rights of all animals evolves naturally from our first emotional connection with nonhuman animals. *The Animal Rights Handbook* is designed as a guide to the wide variety of ways you can incorporate your love and respect for animals into your everyday life.

This book was written in response to the growing number of people who want to know more about animal suffering and what they personally can do to make a difference. As a concise overview of animal rights issues, it outlines the threats animals face and the range of humane responses.

The purpose of this book is *not* to tell you how to live your life. Rather, it offers specific advice about how you can integrate ways to help save animal lives into your everyday routines.

The first six chapters examine different aspects of our lifestyles as they affect animals: how we dress and eat, the products we buy, the way we educate our children and relate to our companion animals at home. The beginning of each chapter gives background information about specific areas of animal abuse and exploitation. After that, you'll find some simple, concrete suggestions about what you can do to help save animal lives.

Each chapter also presents an "Animal Awareness" exercise designed to give you a fresh point of view on how your lifestyle affects animals. Some are quizzes that only take a few minutes. Others require an hour or an afternoon of your time. All of them will help you reevaluate your relationship with the animals who share your home, your community, or some other facet of your daily life.

At the end of each chapter there's a list of resources where you can get more information. Addresses are listed in Chapter Eight, the "Animal Rights Directory." Names and addresses of animal rights organizations and some of the companies that offer compassionate alternatives are also sprinkled throughout the book. If you want more complete and up-to-date information about cruelty-free products, please contact the groups listed at the end of the chapters or in the "Animal Rights Directory" (Chapter Eight).

Chapter Seven, "Speaking Out for Animal Rights," is an introduction to the broad range of groups working for animal rights. No matter what your special area of interest might be, you can be sure that some group shares that focus. And while this book emphasizes the importance of individual action, it is difficult to overestimate the power of collective action in effecting sweeping social change.

The Animal Rights Handbook is an overview of animal suffering and workable human solutions. It's a starting point in an ongoing process of education and change. We hope you'll find it a useful map—whether you're just starting out or are well advanced on your journey down the path of compassionate living.

chapter one

FASHION WITH COMPASSION

FASHION
WITH COMPASSION

Cruelty is one fashion statement we can all do without.
> —Rue McClanahan, actress

I f you want to understand how deeply animal cruelty is embedded in our society and lifestyles, just peek into the average bedroom closet. That fur coat once graced the backs of dozens of wild foxes. Those leather shoes were once the living skin of a cow. That wool sweater once kept a sheep warm in winter.

To put it simply, one thousand generations after emerging from caves, most of us still dress in animal skins!

But take heart. The very presence of animal products in your closets puts the power to *protect* animals squarely in your individual hands. What you choose to put on in the morning is a life and death decision for many creatures in the animal kingdom. Indeed, in the case of clothing derived from exotic and endangered animals, your fashion "statements" can spell the difference between survival and extinction for an entire species.

Only in the past few decades have we begun seriously to question our right to kill animals for clothing. Today, a dead animal draped across one's shoulders looks more barbaric than chic. Ivory earrings and bracelets evoke images of African elephants butchered by poachers. Even leather jackets don't seem as cool as they did when Marlon Brando rode around on a motorcycle.

People have now become aware that the power to destroy can be transformed into the power to save. And with the advent of dozens of new synthetic materials, we are witnessing a veritable revolution in apparel alternatives.

Today we have a clear choice between cruel and compassionate clothing.

And that choice counts. Today's worldwide fashion marketplace is intensely responsive to consumer demand. If you and I refuse to run out and buy this season's offerings, rest assured they won't be back next season. Witness the quick death of midi dresses and bubble skirts. When people started waking up to the cruelty of the fur industry, fashion designers suddenly discovered the advantages of fake fur. Where once it was difficult to find a well-made pair of nonleather shoes, now shoe designers are coming out with smart-looking espadrilles, synthetic dress and casual shoes, and nonleather athletic shoes. And for people who prefer not to wear wool, the cotton alternatives are endless.

As consumers, we have the final say on what we wear. It's the simple law of supply and demand. If we demand fashion without animal cruelty, alternatives will appear on the market. But to make intelligent and compassionate choices, we must first become informed shoppers.

FACTS ABOUT FUR

Trapping

If you wear fur, or if you're considering it, you should know that buying a fur coat made from trapped animals means taking the lives of dozens of creatures. And every one of those animals suffers severe pain in the process.

➤ An estimated 17 million raccoons, beavers, bobcats, lynx, coyotes, muskrats, nutria, and other animals are trapped each year in the United States for fur.

➤ Animals that are caught in spring-loaded steel leg-hold traps (which are now banned in more than 70 countries, as well as in Florida, Rhode Island, and New Jersey) suffer an average of 15 hours of pain before their lives are ended by a trapper's club.

➤ Steel-jawed traps are so painful that many animals chew

ANIMAL AWARENESS

Take a tour of your closet. Go through your shoes, coats, and clothing, and put aside all the items made from animals—that includes leather, wool, down, and of course fur. Now go through the items and imagine a nonanimal replacement for each one. Would a flannel-lined jean jacket work as well as a leather jacket? Would a soft, warm cotton sweater be as nice to wear as wool? Could a well-made pair of synthetic shoes substitute for the leather ones?

The point is not to throw away half the clothes in your closet, but simply to become aware of how many clothes you have that come from animals. You might think about which articles could be substituted with nonanimal products in your next purchase.

By taking inventory of your wardrobe, you can clarify where you draw the line about wearing animal materials. Maybe you want to continue wearing leather but could do without those fur-lined gloves. Giving up clothing made from animals doesn't have to be a hardship. Treat yourself to something wonderful next time you're shop-ping, but something that isn't made from animals!

through their own limbs to escape. These crippled animals often die from infection, loss of blood, or starvation.

➤ For every "target" fur-bearing animal trapped, two non-target animals are caught and killed. Trappers call these animals—such as dogs, cats, deer, and birds of prey—"trash animals."

➤ It takes many more animals to make a fur coat than you may realize. To make a 40-inch coat, depending on the type, it takes 16 coyotes or 18 lynx or 60 mink, 45 opossums, 20 otters, 42 foxes, 40 raccoons, 50 sables, 8 seals, 50 muskrats, or 15 beavers. Add the number of "trash animals" caught, and the toll per coat becomes truly appalling.

Some fur-wearers will argue that trapping is a valuable means of managing wildlife. But scientists and wildlife managers have shown that populations of different wild animals naturally keep each other in balance. Trapping predators and other species disrupts this equilibrium by eliminating key components of an ecosystem. And since it's usually the healthy animals who get caught (sick ones move around too little) trapping weakens the population and endangers many species.

Fur farms

Nearly $2 billion worth of furs were sold in the United States in 1988. Most of those furs came from animals raised for slaughter on fur farms. Perhaps "fur farms" conjures up an image of wide-open country ranches where animals live a happy outdoor existence until their deaths. In fact, most animals raised on fur ranches spend their lives in cramped, miserable conditions.

➤ Animals raised on fur farms, mostly mink and foxes which ordinarily roam widely in their natural habitat, are confined inside tiny wire-mesh cages for their whole lives.

➤ Caged mink are so deprived of normal activity that they often are driven to self-mutilation and pathological repetition of behavior.

➤ Animals on fur farms suffer from stress, fear, disease, and parasites caused by crowded and dirty conditions. In 1987, U.S. mink farmers reported that 450,000 animals died of heat stress on their farms.

➤ Furriers breed animals especially to get the "best" pelt.

This inbreeding often causes physical and behavioral abnormalities.

➤ Since most furriers are primarily interested in profits, they usually kill the animals in the cheapest way possible, which is often also the cruelest. Neck-breaking, suffocation, poisoning, gassing, and electrocution are the most common, and most painful, techniques used.

➤ Persian lambs, whose coats uncurl at fives weeks of age, are skinned within a month of birth so that the curl doesn't go out of their coats.

WHAT YOU CAN DO

Don't wear fur! If everyone chose *not* to buy fur-lined gloves this year, tens of thousands of animal lives would be spared.

Wear a fabulous fake fur, if you must have a coat that looks like fur. So many people are recognizing the cruelty that fur stands for that many top designers are making *faux* fur a fashion statement. In a Milan fashion show, designer Giorgio Armani's plush *faux* furs had labels that read, "Thank you, Giorgio, for saving our skins." Bill Blass, Carolina Herrera, Oleg Cassini, and Norma Kamali are other designers who no longer use fur.

Don't shop at department stores with fur boutiques. Write to the managers to let them know that you oppose the inhumane treatment of animals.

Speak out against fur. You can write to People for the Ethical Treatment of Animals (PETA) for a "Fur Is Dead" Action Pack, which includes a T-shirt, bumper sticker, anti-fur cards to educate fur wearers, fact sheets, and fliers to start your own anti-fur campaign. Send $15 to PETA at P.O. Box 42516, Washington, DC 20015-0516.

Support legislation to ban cruel leg-hold traps. Write to The American Society for the Prevention of Cruelty to

Animals (ASPCA), 441 East 92nd St., New York, NY 10128, or call 212-876-7700 for information about currently pending legislation.

Donate to an organization, such as the ASPCA, the Humane Society of the United States (HSUS), Friends of Animals (FOA), or PETA, to help it place anti-fur ads and billboards, and pursue anti-fur, anti-trapping legislation.

WHO NEEDS THOSE BLUE SUEDE SHOES?

Leather

Leather dominates our wardrobes and lifestyles like no other animal product. It's long been a symbol of style and luxury in clothes and accessories, from boots and jackets to couches and car seats. Leather isn't likely to disappear from our lives overnight, but it's about time we examine the high cost, to animals, of all those gloves, belts, and briefcases.

Most leather comes from the skins of cattle slaughtered for meat or from cows that are no longer able to produce milk. Leather is a direct product of the cruel factory-farming industry that mass-produces animals at the lowest cost for the largest possible profit. (See Chapter Three for more on factory farming.)

➤ Leather is tanned with toxic chemicals, which find their way into streams and rivers, polluting them and killing wildlife.

Wool and down

Wool is sheep's clothing . . . on a human back. Wool production for human wear doesn't require killing sheep, but many shearing procedures are inhumane.

➤ Sheep are bred to have such unnaturally thick fleece that many die of heat exhaustion in summer and exposure in the winter after shearing.

➤ Many sheep are subjected to painful tail-docking, castration, ear-punching, and hurtful shearing methods.

➤ Down feathers are often plucked from living geese, which have sensitive skin.

Endangered and exotic animal products

➤ International consumer demand for ivory products has driven the African elephant to the brink of extinction (and the walrus may be soon to follow). Unless we stop buying ivory jewelry and other ivory products, *today*, the African elephant will be gone by the end of the century. (See Chapter Six, "Let Wildlife Live," for more about elephants and other threatened wildlife.)

➤ Sea turtles are also endangered. But that hasn't stopped

★ SUCCESS STORIES ★

★ Harrods, the famous and fashionable London store, announced in March 1990 that it would close its fur salon. "It's just not the done thing to wear a fur coat in public anymore," the Harrods spokesperson explained. "Harrods has to move with the times."

★ Anti-fur residents of the chic skiing town of Aspen, Colorado, managed to get a citywide fur ban on a voter referendum in 1990. Although the ban was voted down, it received strong support from the mayor and focused international media attention on the fur issue. Next time, a victory!

★ Many top fashion photographers, models, and model agency presidents have pledged never to work with fur again.

★ Fur trade journals report that the "harvest" of wild fur has dropped as much as 80% since anti-fur campaigns began. The three U.S. fur companies with public stock have also reported major losses.

the manufacture of turtle-shell jewelry, combs, and knick-knacks.

WHAT YOU CAN DO

Choose cotton and kindness. Start shopping with an eye for clothes that aren't made from animals. Wear cotton, canvas, linen, nylon, rayon, and other cruelty-free fabrics.

Stay warm with synthetics! Instead of down, buy sleeping bags, ski jackets, and other products filled with Hollofill or another synthetic material. They can be just as warm as down, last longer, cost less, and are usually machine washable.

Don't buy those cruel shoes. Use your imagination when you buy shoes; they don't have to be made from leather. You can buy fashionable canvas shoes, such as espadrilles, or satin flats for evening wear. Kenneth Cole, for example, makes a wonderful line of synthetic shoes that are comfortable, stylish, and well made. Nike, New Balance, Asics, Hush Puppies, Thom McAn, Fayva, and Naturalizer all manufacture nonleather shoes.

Shop cruelty-free at home. Many catalogues, including Carroll Reed, Talbot's, Avon Fashions, Land's End, Banana Republic, and Appleseed's carry nonleather shoes. Certain mail-order catalogues specialize in leather-free wallets, belts, shoes, and accessories. Some we found are:

Aesop Unlimited, 55 Fenno St., P.O. Box 315, N. Cambridge, MA 02140

The Compassionate Consumer, P.O. Box 27, Jericho, NY 11753

Heartland Products, Box 218, Dakota City, IA 50529

Life Stride, Brown Shoe Co., P.O. Box 354, St. Louis, MO 63166

Old Pueblo Traders, P.O. Box 27800, Tucson, AZ 85726

FOR MORE INFORMATION

(See Chapter Eight, the "Animal Rights Directory," for addresses and phone numbers.)

American Society for the Prevention of Cruelty to Animals (ASPCA). Fur fact sheets.

Beauty Without Cruelty. *Compassionate Shopper* (newsletter).

Friends of Animals. *The Agony of Fur* (pamphlet).

The Humane Society of the United States (HSUS). *Close-up Report* on fur.

People for the Ethical Treatment of Animals (PETA). Fact sheets on wool manufacturing, leather, and fur. *PETA News*, September/October 1989.

chapter two

LET YOUR CONSCIENCE DO THE SHOPPING

LET YOUR CONSCIENCE DO THE SHOPPING

Mercy to animals means mercy to mankind.
— Henry Bergh, 1866
Founder, The American Society for the
Prevention of Cruelty to Animals

W're used to thinking about what personal care and household products will do *for us*, whether they'll make our clothes brighter or our hair more manageable. But given the animal suffering that goes into making most "new" and "improved" products, we have to start thinking about what product testing has done *to others*.

The animals that are used in product testing, often without anesthetics or analgesics, suffer every bit as much as would your companion animal at home. You wouldn't force your dog to drink shampoo to find out how toxic it is. So why do we let companies perform those kinds of tests on dogs, rabbits, mice, and other animals?

In a typical year, some 14 million animals suffer and die in laboratory tests to determine the safety of cosmetics and household products for humans. Yet these tests, which may involve blinding, poisoning, and killing of animals, are usually not required by law.

The Food and Drug Administration asks manufacturers only to substantiate that their products are safe, either by using ingredients that are already known to be safe or by testing new additives through any number of means, many of which don't involve animals. Corporations that don't use alternative testing methods are subjecting animals to needless pain and death.

But animal testing isn't just cruel and unnecessary, it's

bad science. What harms a mouse or rabbit may not harm a human, and what's safe for a laboratory animal may make you or me ill when we use it at home. According to Dr. Herbert Gundersheimer of the Physicians Committee for Responsible Medicine, "Results of animal tests are not transferable between species, and therefore cannot guarantee product safety for humans." Many alternative tests—using tissue cultures, human patch tests, or computer models—have proven to be as or more reliable than those using animals.

There is no clearer case of needless and preventable animal cruelty than product testing. Fortunately, if you care about animals, there is a simple solution: stop buying products that have been tested on animals. Over the past few years, boycotts organized by animal rights activists have helped persuade several major cosmetic companies to switch to tests that don't involve animals. So there are plenty of cruelty-free alternatives for you to choose from, whether it's laundry detergent or top-of-the-line perfume.

And by buying only cruelty-free products, you send a strong message to companies that still test on animals: stop the testing, or lose sales.

TEST RESULTS: TOXIC TO ANIMALS

If you haven't made an effort to buy cruelty-free products, it's likely that almost everything in your kitchen and bathroom—your bath soap and baby powder, sink cleanser and laundry detergent, mascara and makeup—was tested on animals. Here are some of the most common tests conducted on animals.

➤ *The Draize Eye Irritancy Test*, invented in 1944, is the standard method companies use to test cosmetics and household products for eye irritation. Rabbits are used most often in these tests, because they have no tear ducts and cannot shed tears that would dilute the chemicals (and relieve the pain). Concentrated solutions of a product are

ANIMAL AWARENESS

Take a good hard look at the household cleansers stored under your kitchen and bathroom sinks. Take out all the bottles, aerosol cans, and spray pumps and line them up on the counter. First read the labels on the front. You'll probably see lots of claims like NEW & IMPROVED! ADVANCED FORMULA! INDUSTRIAL STRENGTH CLEANER!

Now turn the bottles around and read the back labels. You know, the parts they never read aloud on the television commercials: WARNING—May burn eyes and skin! POISON: If swallowed induce vomiting immediately. KEEP AWAY FROM CHILDREN AND PETS!

Barraged by nonstop media hype urging us to buy the newest and most efficient products, we may never stop to consider a simple, sad fact: every toxic, poisonous product we bring into our homes was "tested" on dozens or hundreds of animals. Every "new" and "improved" ingredient means a new round of toxic testing on animals.

Now here's the good news. In the 1990s it's easy to have a toxic-free, cruelty-free household. In this chapter we list dozens of companies that specialize in cruelty-free, nontoxic products. And for more tips on how to have a toxic-free home, you can read *Nontoxic, Natural & Earthwise*, by Debra Lynn Dadd (Jeremy Tarcher Inc., 1990). After you've replaced all those skull and crossbone warnings with cruelty-free labels, your home won't just be more humane. It will be a lot safer, too.

dripped into the rabbit's eyes. The damage is measured according to the animal's swelling, redness, and injury. Because rabbits would normally shut or claw their eyes to remove the offending substances, they are either immobilized in stocks or their eyes are held open by the use of metal clips. After the tests, the rabbits are killed.

For years many physicians and humane organizations have been calling for a ban on the Draize test—not only because it causes animal suffering but also because scientists have found it to be unreliable. Certain substances cause no reactions to rabbits' eyes, even at high concentrations, but can cause pain and irritation in humans. Other products make it to the market despite the fact that they were Draize-tested and found to be irritants. There seems to be little scientific purpose for the Draize test—or for the animal suffering.

➤ *The LD50 test* ("lethal dose 50%") is usually performed by force-feeding a product to several groups of animals until half the animals in one group die. At the conclusion of the test, the surviving animals—those that suffer but don't die—are killed or used in another test.

Scientists have found that the LD50 test, for all the pain and cruelty it inflicts on animals, is hardly a foolproof measure of how safe a product is for humans. In 1982, the National Society for Medical Research (NSMR) issued a statement: "It is the opinion of the NSMR that the routine use of the quantitative LD50 test is not now scientifically justified." Yet many companies still continue what one toxicologist has called "the ritual mass execution of animals."

➤ Numerous other kinds of cruel tests are performed on animals. Skin irritancy tests, for example, are performed by removing the hair from animals, usually by applying strong adhesive tape and rapidly ripping it off. Then irritants are applied to the skin and covered with another patch of adhesive tape.

ALTERNATIVES TO ANIMAL TESTS

Many scientists support the development of humane, nonanimal methods of testing products, although they don't always agree on which alternatives are most viable. At the very least, alternative methods can drastically decrease the number of animal tests conducted and the number of animals used in those tests.

Here are some current alternatives to animal tests.

➤ *Computer programs* have been developed to simulate the LD50 test; information from humans is used to predict the toxicity of new products.

➤ *Human skin patch tests*, or tests using egg membranes and tissue cultures, can replace the Draize and skin irritancy tests.

➤ *Cell culture tests* are replacing the Draize test at many companies. These tests are faster, more accurate, and much more cost-efficient.

➤ *Organic ingredients* are used by many companies instead of toxic chemicals. Numerous ingredients known to be safe can be used in products without ever having to be tested.

ANIMAL ADDITIVES

In addition to being tested on animals, many cosmetics contain animal-derived ingredients. These products aren't cruelty-free either. Always read labels to see if they contain a pledge that the product was not tested on animals. Also check for hidden animal ingredients.

➤ *Hydrolized animal collagen*, used in some shampoos, is purified animal fat. Lipsticks and other cosmetics may contain animal proteins.

➤ *Lanolin* is an animal by-product that is frequently added to lotions and shampoos. Other animal by-products include animal proteins, placenta, and urea.

➤ *Beeswax, honey, milk, or eggs* are a few animal-derived

products found in many "natural" cosmetics; you may want to avoid them if you're very careful about not using animal products.

WHAT YOU CAN DO

Use cruelty-free products

There are over 150 cruelty-free companies that don't use animal testing or animal ingredients in their products. (Aubrey Organics, Aveda, Beauty Without Cruelty USA, Dr. E. H. Bronner, Earth Science, JLM Enterprises, Jojoba Farms, Kiss My Face, KMS, Nexxus, Sleepy Hollow, Tom's of Maine, and Waleda are just a few examples.) Their products often display a label stating that they weren't tested on animals. When in doubt, do some research.

Lists of cruelty-free product lines are continually being updated as animal rights activists persuade more and more companies to stop testing on animals. You can get current lists by writing to these organizations:

The American Society for the Prevention of Cruelty to Animals (ASPCA), 441 East 92nd St., New York, NY 10128

Beauty Without Cruelty USA, 175 West 12th St., #15G, New York, NY 10011-8275

Coalition to End Animal Suffering and Exploitation (CEASE), P.O. Box 27, Cambridge, MA 02238

People for the Ethical Treatment of Animals (PETA), P.O. Box 42516, Washington, DC 20015-0516

Shopper's Guide to Cruelty-Free Products, Animal Protection Institute of America, P.O. Box 22505, Sacramento, CA 95822

Several companies make household products that are not tested on animals. If you can't find their brands (or other cruelty-free brands) in your neighborhood store, call or write to them to find out where they're available. And ask your local store manager to stock their products.

Alba Botanica, P.O. Box 12085, Santa Rosa, CA 95406, 707-575-3111. Laundry, dishwashing, and cleansing liquids.

Baudelaire, Inc., Forest Road, Marlow, NH 03456, 603-352-9234. Cruelty-free imported body care products.

Bon Ami, 1025 West 8th St., Kansas City, MO 64101, 816-842-2939. Polishing cleanser, available in many supermarkets.

The Body Shop, Hanover Technical Center, 45 Horsehill Road, Cedar Knolls, NJ 07927-2003, 201-984-9200. Cruelty-free body care products.

Dr. E. H. Bronner, P.O. Box 28, Escondido, CA 92033, 619-743-2211. Soaps and liquid organic cleanser, available at many health food stores and drugstores.

Home Service Products Co., 230 Willow St., Bound Brook, NJ 08805, 201-348-2393. Laundry soap, dishwashing detergent, and fabric softener.

Huish Chemical, 3540 West, 1987 South, Salt Lake City, UT 84125, 801-972-8611. Laundry detergent.

The Murphy Phoenix Co., 258 Science Park Dr., Beachwood, OH 44122, 216-831-0404. Murphy's Oil Soap, available at many supermarkets.

Sierra Dawn, 1814 Emprie Industrial Ct., #D, Santa Rosa, CA 95474, 707-577-0324. Household products, biodegradable camping soap, cleanser, laundry detergent, fabric cleaner, fine washable soap, and others.

Shop at home for cruelty-free products

If you live in an area where few stores stock cruelty-free products, take heart. Numerous mail-order houses cater to the compassionate consumer. Not only can you buy these products, but you can do it without having to spend time hunting for them in stores. The "Animal Rights Directory" in Chapter Eight provides a long list of mail-order catalogues you can write away for.

Make your own household cleaners

You can create your own alternatives to chemical products by using common, safe, and inexpensive ingredients that are probably sitting on your kitchen shelf. The book *Home Ecology*, by Karen Christiansen (Fulcrum Publishing, 1990) has recipes for homemade cleaning products.

Boycott animal-tested products

Boycotts can be the best means of converting individual buying power into forceful collective action. Economic boycotts have proven to be potent instruments of social change, both in the civil rights and animal rights movements.

The groups listed on page 23 can provide you with current lists of companies that test their products on animals. You may choose to avoid buying those companies' products. And if you want to have even greater impact, call or write the companies and let them know why you no longer buy their products. The names, addresses, and toll-free consumer phone line numbers of major personal care product manufacturers are listed in the "Animal Rights Directory" in the back of this book. Be sure to check with the groups on page 23 to find out which of these companies currently test on animals before you write or call to protest.

Be a stockholder activist. If you own stock in a company that conducts animal testing, you can voice complaints to the company at its stockholders' meetings. Contact PETA in Washington, D.C., to become part of their corporate responsibility project, or call the ASPCA in New York City at 212-876-7700 for more information on how to be a conscientious stockholder.

Support cruelty-free laws. Legislation concerning animal testing is usually pending in Congress. The Consumer

Products Safe Testing Act, for example, is a bill that would prohibit lethal-dose tests and encourage alternatives. Write to your representative or senators to ask them to support humane legislation. The address is U.S. House of Representatives, Washington, DC 20515, or U.S. Senate, Washington, DC 20510. For up-to-date information about pending legislation, contact the ASPCA, the Humane Society of the United States (HSUS), PETA, or other national animal rights groups (see Chapter Eight).

ANIMALS AND MEDICAL RESEARCH

More than any other issue, the use of animals in laboratory research has galvanized the animal rights movement. Subjecting nonhuman animals to extreme pain and death for the sake of human health is seen by many people as the ultimate expression of humankind's exploitation of animals.

The use of animals in medical research is a complex moral issue. Virtually all animal protection groups are united in their desire to limit or eliminate animals in research. But there exists honest (and heated) disagreement over goals in this area, as well as over tactics for achieving those goals.

Some animal advocates argue that animal testing is never justified. Others fear that completely eliminating animals from research might threaten the lives of people suffering from now-incurable diseases, such as AIDS or heart disease. Most animal activists agree that responsible animal testing for medical purposes should be used if, and only if, there are no alternatives and the knowledge sought is absolutely essential. In those exceptional cases, the fewest number of animals necessary for scientific validity should be used, they should be given the best physical and psychological care possible, and further research into nonanimal alternatives should accompany the investigation.

The immediate abolition of animal research is simply not a realistic goal, given the enormity of the animal research industry. If we hope to work toward a day when no animal is used in research, we must begin by reforming the system that now victimizes tens of millions of animals every year.

The most effective legal tool for regulating animal care in laboratories has been the Animal Welfare Act. Passed by Congress in 1966 and amended several times since, it requires the licensing of laboratories, sets standards for animal care, and mandates both lab inspections by the U.S. Department of Agriculture and the oversight of research protocols by Institutional Animal Care and Use Committees (IACUCs). The problem has been implementation and enforcement in the face of heavy lobbying by the research industry. Over time, however, the vigilance of animal rights groups has paid off. After a three-year court battle, improved regulations were finally released by the Department of Agriculture in 1989.

There are countless examples of animal experiments that proved nothing except that human beings can be the cruelest of all animals: studies of head trauma in which skulls of cats and monkeys were crushed; addiction studies in which animals were force-fed drugs and then underwent withdrawal or killed themselves in their frenzy; military-funded experiments that used animals to see what bullet wounds and chemical warfare agents do to living creatures; electric shock experiments on monkeys, rats, and other animals; and painful tests of every sort, usually without analgesia. These kinds of experiments are simply torturous and inhumane.

As with product testing, numerous alternative methods have proved effective replacements for animal experiments:

➤ Tissue culture tests have been used in AIDS research to isolate, identify, and concentrate the AIDS virus and are being used to rapidly test drugs to see if they work against the virus.

➤ X rays were developed without using animals.

➤ The discovery of penicillin and its effect on infectious diseases was made without using animals.

➤ The vaccine against yellow fever was discovered without animals.

➤ Since 1986, the National Cancer Institute (NCI) has reduced its use of animals from 6 million to fewer than 300,000 a year. The NCI's anti-tumor drug discovery program, which uses human tumor cells instead of animals, will be faster, more dependable, and more cost-effective than using animals.

WHAT YOU CAN DO

If you are concerned about animal experimentation, you can get involved with a group working to reform or eliminate it (see Chapter Eight for names and addresses). If you contribute to a disease-prevention research group, ask them about their policy on animal testing. For technical and medical information about animal experimentation, the Physicians Committee for Responsible Medicine, the Association of Veterinarians for Animal Rights, and Psychologists for the Ethical Treatment of Animals can provide you with the most up-to-date scientific perspectives. You can also write to your legislators, asking them to vote against spending tax dollars on useless and cruel animal experiments.

Unfortunately, the biomedical research community is less vulnerable to individual consumer action than cosmetic and household product manufacturers. But you can still personally do something to help relieve animal suffering in labs.

Donate your organs or body to scientific research. An adequate supply of human organs and cadavers will reduce the numbers of animals used for organ transplants, tissue research, and anatomy study.

Serve on a local Institutional Animal Care and Use Committee (IACUC). IACUCs are mandated by the Animal Welfare Act to review all federally funded research using animals. While you should be prepared to deal with a faculty panel that supports animal research, you can help

★ SUCCESS STORIES ★

★ One of the early successes in the animal rights movement was getting some major cosmetics companies to try alternatives to the Draize test. In 1980, the Coalition to Stop Draize Rabbit Blinding Tests took out a full-page ad in the *New York Times* and several other newspapers, asking, "How many rabbits does Revlon blind for beauty's sake?" The group, dressed in bunny costumes, demonstrated in front of Revlon's corporate headquarters. The campaign grew to international proportions, and eventually Revlon made an offer to grant $750,000 to Rockefeller University to carry out a search for alternative tests. Soon, Avon and Estee Lauder also supported research for alternatives.

★ Since animal advocates have been pressuring cosmetics companies to stop testing on animals, many companies have announced a phase-out of their animal testing, including Avon, Elizabeth Arden, Charles of the Ritz, Max Factor, Revlon, Faberge, Amway, and Shaklee.

★ After a scathing parody in Berke Breathed's "Bloom County" comic strip, the Mary Kay cosmetics company instituted a moratorium on animal testing.

★ The Body Shop, a British-based company dedicated to cruelty-free body care products, has grown from a storefront start-up fourteen years ago to a $141 million worldwide business.

ensure that all appropriate regulations are enforced and that alternatives to animal use are considered.

Investigate the open meeting or "sunshine" laws in your community. Many municipalities require that meetings about publicly funded projects be open to the public. The ASPCA and the Animal Legal Defense Fund have successfully sued state-run universities to open their IACUC meetings to the public.

FOR MORE INFORMATION

American Society for the Prevention of Cruelty to Animals (ASPCA). "A Question of Respect," a video on the use of animals in research, testing, and education, and available alternatives. Available through Varied Directions, P.O. Box 1057, Camden, ME 04843.

Animal Protection Institute of America. "Product Testing: A Way Without Animals" (pamphlet).

Coalition to End Animal Suffering and Exploitation (CEASE). *Greater Boston & New England Guide to Compassionate Living.*

People for the Ethical Treatment of Animals (PETA). *The PETA Guide to Compassionate Living* and fact sheets: "Companies That Don't Test on Animals," "Alternative Methods: Healing Without Hurt," and "Cosmetic Testing: Toxic and Tragic."

Physicians Committee for Responsible Medicine. *Beyond the Draize Test.*

Henry Spira. "Fighting to Win," in *In Defense of Animals*, ed. Peter Singer. Harper & Row, 1985.

chapter three

LOVE ANIMALS, DON'T EAT THEM

LOVE ANIMALS, DON'T EAT THEM

Animals are my friends . . . and I don't eat my friends.
—George Bernard Shaw

In an average lifetime, a meat-eating American will consume 1 calf, 3 lambs, 11 cows, 23 hogs, 45 turkeys, 1,097 chickens, and 15,665 chicken eggs.

And yet it's possible to spend that entire lifetime without ever confronting the reality of what (or whom) we're eating. That's no accident. The food industry—from supermarkets to restaurants to advertisers—conspires to keep us at a safe distance from the original source of our meals. They understand that the average consumer is more comfortable with the idea of enjoying hot dogs, hamburgers, and veal cutlets than the reality of eating pigs, cows, and baby calves. Even the term "meat" is a kinder label than "dead animal."

The sad fact is that 95% of the animals we eat are bred for slaughter in cramped, unnatural, and unhealthy conditions. Our "steaks" and "chops" aren't born in sanitized plastic wrapping at the local supermarket. They were once living, breathing creatures who were, for the most part, raised for profit on cruel, mechanized factory farms.

Certainly, you can care about animals without being a vegetarian. But you owe it to yourself to make an informed decision about your diet based on a clear understanding of how your food was raised, killed, and packaged. And whether you are a meat-eater or a vegetarian, the suffering of animals on factory farms demands redress.

A great deal of scientific evidence says that we shouldn't be eating animals. Studies of vegetarians have shown that they're a lot healthier than meat-eaters. And environmental organizations have documented how our carnivorous habits are wreaking havoc on the earth's natural resources. There are numerous arguments on both sides about whether humans were meant to be carnivorous or are simply wayward vegetarians. But that debate is really beside the point.

The best reason to stop eating meat is the simplest one: to end the exploitation and killing of animals. And because the meat industry, like any other business, lives by the law of supply and demand, you can personally and directly reduce animal suffering by not eating meat. Whether you decide to simply give up eating cows and sheep—or whether you also stop eating poultry, fish, and dairy products—your daily choice of foods will make an important difference.

ON THE FACTORY FARM

Popular mythology would have you believe that animals raised for meat live on an Old MacDonald's Farm of green pastures and wide-open barnyards, well fed and well cared for until the day they're taken to the slaughterhouse.

That may once have been the case, but farm life isn't a storybook setting these days. Most of the red meat and virtually all the poultry products we eat are produced in large, production-oriented factory farms. Animals are crowded into pens and cages and fed large amounts of antibiotics to counter the diseases that run rampant under those conditions. Often subjected to cruel confinement, factory-farm animals are treated more like machine parts on an assembly line than sentient creatures who feel and suffer pain.

Chickens

Raising chickens has become a precisely automated science. Chickens are raised to be "breeders" or "layers." Of the type that lay eggs, all the male chicks (an estimated 240 million a year) are killed shortly after hatching because they

ANIMAL AWARENESS

Next time you visit your local supermarket, stop at the meat counter and take a close look at the labels. Everyone knows that "drumstick" is a fancy word for a chicken's leg, but can you identify what part of a cow the following items are cut from?

1. filet mignon
2. chateaubriand
3. Delmonico
4. T-bone
5. sirloin tip

6. chuck steak
7. sweetbreads
8. flank
9. shank
10. prime rib

Answers: 1-E, 2-I, 3-J, 4-A, 5-C, 6-D, 7-G, 8-B, 9-H, 10-F

If you eat meat and identified fewer than half of the items, you probably know less about your food than you thought. Next time you buy meat, ask your butcher which part of the cow your steak is cut from. Here are some other questions you might want answered: Where was the cow born and raised? How was it slaughtered, and at what age? What was it fed? Did its diet include hormones? Antibiotics?

Once you learn about how that cow lived and died, you may want to give its brothers and sisters a break!

are useless to the factory production. The hens are kept in stacked wire-mesh cages, where conveyor belts bring in food and water and carry away eggs and excrement. Because they're subjected to so much stress that they may peck each other to death, the hens are painfully debeaked with hot irons. After about a year, when their productivity wanes, the factory farmer often uses forced moulting, which shocks the birds into renewed egg productivity for another few months. When the hens can no longer produce, they are delivered to "processors" to be turned into soup stock or frozen foods.

"Broiler" chickens are raised in windowless sheds where lighting is manipulated to force them to eat as often as possible. These chickens are also debeaked, which can make it painful for them to eat and drink due to severe blisters and sores in their mouths. The same hot-knife machine that debeaks the birds also clips their claws to prevent them from fighting and cuts off the males' wattles and combs. These chickens are killed after just nine weeks.

➤ 20% of hens raised in factory farms die of stress or disease.

➤ 80% of all poultry are given antibiotics.

➤ Half of all chickens sold in the United States are infected with a toxic bacteria called salmonella, according to *The New York Times*. Up to 4 million Americans are believed to contract salmonella poisoning each year.

Pigs

The average factory-farm pig may never see daylight until the day he or she is transported to the market. Sows are usually restricted to dark, narrow stalls where they can only stand or lie down. They are continually bred with boars or artificially inseminated to produce the maximum number of litters.

After a sow gives birth, she is confined to a stall. There, she can only eat, drink, and keep her teats exposed to her baby pigs. After the pigs are born, their tails are cut off, their ears are notched, their needle teeth are clipped, and the males are castrated—all without anesthetic. When it's time for the sow to go back to the breeding area, her little pigs are moved to "finishing buildings," where they spend 20 weeks in darkness until they reach market weight.

➤ 70% of all pigs are constantly confined during their lives.

➤ Approximately 30% of all pork products are contaminated with toxoplasmosis, a disease caused by parasites that can be passed on to consumers.

Cows

Cattle don't roam the range contentedly chewing on grasses until it's time for slaughter. Often they are raised in crowded conditions and fed an unnatural diet of high-bulk fillers, including sawdust, to get them to their desired weight. They are usually castrated, dehorned, and branded without anesthetics. Frequently transported in metal trucks, where they often get sick and injured from crowding and extreme temperatures, they go from one location to another for fattening and slaughter.

Dairy cows are constantly manipulated in order to maintain a profitable flow of milk. They are always either pregnant or nursing to produce milk. They are often dosed with hormones—which can cause shock or death—to tune their reproductive systems to the factory's schedule and to decrease the time between pregnancies.

➤ Cattle lose up to 9% of their body weight while being transported.

➤ 60% of all cattle are given antibiotics regularly.

➤ 55% of all U.S. antibiotics are fed to livestock—a total of more than 2,000 different drugs and chemicals.

Calves

Veal calves receive the harshest treatment of all factory-farm animals. Newly born male calves (who are useless for milk production) are taken from their mothers within days of birth and placed in narrow wooden stalls, where they cannot turn around or lie down in a natural position. In order to prevent muscle development and to speed weight gain, they are not allowed exercise and are kept in almost total darkness to reduce restlessness. They are fed an iron-deficient diet of milky gruel in order to obtain the light-colored meat that gourmets prefer. Because desperate calves will attempt to lick their own urine and feces to satisfy their craving for iron, they are chained in their tiny stalls to completely restrict movement.

➤ Respiratory and intestinal diseases and chronic diarrhea run rampant in veal calves.

➤ When veal calves are slaughtered at 16 weeks of age, they are often too sick to walk. One out of every 10 calves dies in confinement.

A MORE BALANCED DIET—AND ENVIRONMENT

Animals aren't the only victims of factory farming. Our whole environment is suffering as a result of meat production—suffering from overgrazing, water pollution, topsoil erosion, and rainforest destruction. Because so many natural resources are used in meat production, if we stopped producing meat we could greatly decrease our use of fossil fuel and water—both scarce. Finally, we could vastly increase the world's most precious resource—grain—if so much of it weren't fed to livestock.

Nature and natural resources

➤ Agriculture is the leading cause of water pollution in the U.S., most of it due to livestock manure.

➤ Fifty times more fossil fuels are needed to produce a meat-centered diet than a vegetarian diet.

➤ Forests throughout the world are being destroyed to make room for cattle grazing. Between 1960 and 1985,

40% of all Central American rainforests were destroyed to create pasture for beef cattle.

➤ An acre of trees is spared each year for every individual who switches to a meatless diet.

➤ The production of a pound of beef requires 2,500 gallons of water. More than half of all water used in the United States goes to livestock production.

➤ It takes less water to feed a total vegetarian for a year than a meat-eater for a month.

Human hunger

➤ It takes 16 pounds of grain to produce a pound of beef. The U.S. livestock population consumes enough grain and soybeans each year to feed more than five times the entire U.S. population: 1.3 billion people.

➤ If Americans reduced their meat consumption by only 10%, there would be 12 million more tons of grain to feed humans, enough to feed each of the 60 million people who starve to death each year.

➤ One acre of pasture produces about 165 pounds of beef, but the same acre can produce 20,000 pounds of potatoes.

Health concerns

It's a myth that you need to eat red meat to be strong and healthy. In fact, there's plenty of evidence that vegetarians are much healthier than meat-eaters. Eating meat has been linked to heart disease, cancer, diabetes, arthritis, and osteoporosis. Animal fat and cholesterol (found only in animal products) are the leading causes of heart attacks and strokes.

Other health risks are increased by the chemicals, antibiotics, and hormones found in meat. Animals are fed many antibiotics to keep them from getting diseases in dirty, crowded, stressful situations. Because people consume so many unnecessary antibiotics, many new antibiotic-resistant strains of pneumonia, gonorrhea, salmonella, and other illnesses have developed, decreasing our ability to treat those diseases.

Not eating meat, on the other hand, significantly reduces your risk of illness. And it's been found that vegetarians get plenty of protein if they include other sources of protein in their diets, such as tofu and tempeh (or other soy products) and beans and rice.

➤ You can reduce the risk of heart attack by 90% if you eliminate meat, eggs, and dairy products from your diet.

➤ Vegetarians suffer less from osteoporosis than do meat-eaters.

➤ 88% of all pesticide residues in the U.S. diet are contained in meat and dairy products.

➤ Breast milk from mothers who eat meat contains 35 times more pesticide contamination than milk from vegetarian mothers.

➤ A woman who eats meat daily is four times more at risk of breast cancer than a woman who eats meat once a week.

➤ Vegetarians as a group have lower blood pressure than meat-eaters.

WHAT YOU CAN DO

Eat meat less often

The easiest way to prevent needless animal suffering and the harmful environmental effects of meat-eating is to simply cut down on meat. If you do eat meat, for the sake of animals and your health, try to eat animals (or animal by-products) that aren't raised on factory farms.

Gradually give up some meats. Try eating lower on the food chain: fish and dairy, but no poultry or red meat. The book *The Gradual Vegetarian* (listed at the end of this chapter) can help you find meat alternatives.

Eat free-range or organic eggs instead of factory-farm eggs. Not only are they healthier for you, but the chickens live better lives. A group called Food Animals Concerns Trust (FACT) sells "Nest Eggs" from free-range chickens. FACT also markets "Rambling Rose" veal for farmers who raise veal calves humanely.

Shop at your local farmers' markets. Small family farmers almost always use fewer pesticides, antibiotics, and other toxic chemicals. They also don't usually raise animals in cramped factory-farming conditions.

Read the labels in supermarkets, and watch out for the occasional animal products that slip in, like lard, gelatin, and whey, which are often found in desserts and bakery products. Ask your grocer to separate factory-farm and nonfactory-farm foods.

Treat yourself to a wonderful vegetarian meal. Find the best vegetarian restaurant in town, or order a great vegetarian meal at an Indian, Italian, Chinese, Thai, or Cambodian restaurant.

Become a vegetarian

Becoming a vegetarian doesn't mean a life sentence of bland tofu and brown rice. Vegetarians eat a wide variety of healthful, tasty foods. Remember that throughout the world there are nearly as many vegetarians as meat-eaters. And a host of new vegetarian foods are available here at home, ranging from meatless hot dogs to soybean milk.

If you decide to give up meat, you might want to do it gradually, as suggested above. Start by identifying your favorite meatless foods and work from there.

It's important to find some good vegetarian cookbooks for guidance along the way. Fortunately, as vegetarianism becomes more and more widespread, a wealth of creative vegetarian cookbooks is appearing on the market. We've listed a few of our favorites at the end of this chapter. Some of these books will also advise you on how to get plenty of protein and the right nutrients in your diet.

You'll want to take a trip to a health food store to find

out about all the meatless alternatives on the market. Some of the best high-protein substitutes for meat are made from soybeans. Tofu (bean curd), a versatile protein made from soy milk, can be broiled, braised, barbecued, or sauteed. Tempeh is another soybean product that has even more protein and a more meatlike texture. Miso is a fermented soy product that can be used as a soup base or condiment. Other soybean products on the market are more direct substitutes for meat dishes, such as tofu-burgers and "meatless bacon" (or "chicken" or "bologna"). There are also several cheese substitutes made from soy, such as Nu Tofu, that taste as good as the real thing.

Adopting a vegetarian diet is a matter of personal taste. You can be a vegetarian in many different ways. It may be difficult to give up all meat and dairy products because you live somewhere where there are few health food stores, or because your family objects, or because you simply prefer to eat some animal-derived foods. That's fine. You don't have to be a purist to help animals.

Here are a few varieties of vegetarianism:

➤ *Total Vegetarians* eat only plant foods; that is, no animal foods, eggs, or dairy products.

➤ *Vegans* eat only plant foods and avoid wearing or buying products derived from animals, such as wool and leather. (For information on becoming a vegan and buying vegan products, write to Vegan Street, P.O. Box 5525, Rockville, MD 20855.)

➤ *Lacto-Vegetarians* include milk in their diets.

➤ *Lacto-Ovo-Vegetarians* eat dairy products and eggs.

➤ *Pesco-Vegetarians* eat fish but no other meat (many Asians are pesco-vegetarians).

➤ *Pollo-Vegetarians* eat chicken, duck, or turkey but no "red meat."

No matter what type of vegetarian you decide to become, there are a few things to keep in mind.

Teach by example. Don't be surprised if you meet resistance from your meat-and-potato friends and relatives. They may ridicule you and probably won't be persuaded by logic (or preaching). Just remember that the best way to influence others is by example.

★ SUCCESS STORIES ★

★ Intensive factory farming was banned in Sweden in 1988. Grazing rights were guaranteed for cows, larger cages for chickens, and separate bedding and feeding places for pigs.

★ There are now over 15 million vegetarians in the U. S., up from 9 million in 1982. Millions more people have cut down on meat or eat only fish.

★ It's becoming much easier to find vegetarian restaurants. They're often listed in the *Yellow Pages* under "restaurants." Listings of vegetarian restaurants are also available from local vegetarian societies and animal rights groups. The magazine *Vegetarian Times* has a directory of restaurants, as does the Coalition to End Animal Suffering and Exploitation (CEASE). If you're a traveler, *The International Vegetarian Travel Guide* is available through *Vegetarian Times*.

★ Even fast-food restaurants have added more healthful vegetarian alternatives—such as salad bars and baked potatoes—so vegetarians on the road don't have to brown-bag it anymore.

★ When you become a vegetarian, you'll be joining the illustrious company of Socrates, Plato, Leonardo da Vinci, Leo Tolstoy, Sir Isaac Newton, Charles Darwin, George Bernard Shaw, Henry David Thoreau, Gandhi, and, more recently, Paul Newman, Cicely Tyson, Gloria Swanson, Bob Dylan, George Harrison, Ravi Shankar, Gladys Knight, and the B-52s.

Keep trying new recipes and products. Try a tofu-burger (with the works). If you drink milk, try soy milk for a change and see how you like it on your cereal, in your coffee, or in anything you usually cook with milk.

Ask for meatless meals and nonfactory-farm products at restaurants, hotels, airlines, and schools.

VEGETARIAN COOKBOOKS

Diet for a Small Planet. Frances Moore Lappé. Ballantine Books, 1971.

The Farm Vegetarian Cookbook. Louise Hagler, ed. The Book Publishing Company, 1978.

The Gradual Vegetarian. Lisa Tracy. Dell, 1985.

Moosewood Cookbook. Mollie Katzen. Ten Speed Press, 1977.

The New Laurel's Kitchen. Laurel Robertson. Ten Speed Press, 1986.

The Vegetarian Epicure. Anna Thomas. Vintage Books, 1972.

Vegetarian Gourmet. Sally and Lucien Berg. McGraw-Hill, 1971.

FOR MORE INFORMATION

American Society for the Prevention of Cruelty to Animals (ASPCA). "The Other Side of the Fence," a video on the veal industry and factory farming. Available for $69.95 through Varied Directions, P.O. Box 1057, Camden, ME 04843.

The Humane Farming Association. *The Dangers of Factory Farming* (booklet) and Campaign Against Factory Farming issues of *Watchdog.*

Mason, Jim. "Brave New Farm," in *In Defense of Animals*, ed. Peter Singer. Harper & Row, 1985.

People for the Ethical Treatment of Animals (PETA). Fact sheets on vegetarianism and factory farming; also a poster, "How to Win an Argument with a Meat Eater."

Physicians Committee for Responsible Medicine. *PCRM Guide to Healthy Eating* (newsletter). Available from PCRM, P.O. Box 6322, Washington, DC 20015.

Robbins, John. *Diet for a New America.* Stillpoint, 1987.

Vegetarian Times (magazine). Write P.O. Box 570, Oak Park, IL 60303. Or call 1-800-435-0715 for subscriptions.

chapter four

YOU'RE A DOG'S BEST FRIEND

YOU'RE A DOG'S BEST FRIEND

I care not much for a man's religion
whose dog and cat are not the better for it.

— Abraham Lincoln

Most of us experience our first and strongest bond with a nonhuman animal when we get close to a dog or a cat. We come to know our companion animal as a friend, and we delight in the unconditional love, comfort, and playfulness he or she brings into our lives.

We Americans are a people who love our pets. We love to take them for walks, buy them toys, feed them treats, and smother them with affection. Yet we're also a nation that allows more than 13 million dogs and cats a year to be put to death. We sit by and watch while domesticated animals overpopulate to the point of massive homelessness. We let unwanted, uncared-for dogs and cats roam the streets hungry. We confine them in small cages until the day comes—after no home can be found—when we put them to death.

Why do we let animals we love so much endure such suffering?

Too often, when we consider the lives of companion animals, we don't look beyond our own backyards. We may let our dog or cat have puppies or kittens, hoping to find them good homes, without thinking about the staggering number of other animals out there who will never have a home. We may not realize that some of those animals will suffer pain and neglect, or even end up being sold to laboratories as research subjects.

Our responsibility for protecting companion animals

should extend beyond our own pets. Even the terms "pet" and "pet owner" betray a materialistic relationship more appropriate to one's car or house than to a sentient being. Legally, a pet is our personal property. But "property" hardly describes these complex bonds, as anyone who has loved an animal knows.

Humans have a special responsibility to companion animals. We domesticated these animals centuries ago, so they are dependent on us for their care. Not only do they need our friendship—they need our protection against mistreatment and abuse. Considering the loyalty and trust they give us so freely, they deserve nothing less in return.

PET SHOPS AND PUPPY MILLS

How much is that doggie in the window? No matter what the cost of the cuddly little puppy in a pet shop, the price—in terms of animal suffering—is most likely far too high. If you're looking for a companion animal, you probably wouldn't want to find her in a pet shop. Here's why:

➤ The majority of the puppies sold in pet shops (about 360,000 a year) are mass-produced in breeding kennels that have been dubbed "puppy mills" because of their inhumane, production-oriented practices.

➤ Many breeding kennels are overcrowded and dirty. Puppies often don't receive adequate nutrition or veterinary care. As a result, many puppies are stressed and sick by the time they reach the pet shop. If you buy a puppy from a pet shop, you may be surprised when, only a few days later, he starts showing signs of ailments that can be very expensive to treat.

➤ The adult female dogs in breeding kennels have a miserable existence, spending their lives confined in metal cages, producing litters continuously from a young age to five or six years old. After her productivity declines, the female dog is usually destroyed.

ANIMAL AWARENESS

The next time you walk past a pet shop, step inside. Take a good look at the animals for sale. How big are the cages? Do they look clean? Observe the animals for a little while. Do they look healthy and content, with lustrous coats and firm skin? Or do they appear to be agitated, depressed, or malnourished?

Ask the pet shop owner where the animals came from and whether they get any exercise and play time. You may discover that these cute little puppies and kittens are really sad, neurotic creatures who've never had the chance to live healthy lives.

Next, take a look at some of the products the pet shop sells. Are they nontoxic? Or do the labels have a lot of chemical names on them? Does the shop offer vegetarian pet food? Does it offer advice on nutrition and veterinary care?

Keep looking until you find a pet shop that doesn't sell animals and offers nontoxic products as well as advice on the care and feeding of your companion animal. When you do find one, go back to the other stores and tell the owners why you've taken your business elsewhere.

➤ From the time they are born to the time they reach the pet shop, puppies have little contact with their mother or with human companions. This lack of love is responsible for the nervous temperaments or the shy, frightened behavior they exhibit in pet shops. Mistreated early on, these pups may later be skittish, bite, yelp constantly, or develop other nervous disorders.

POPULATION EXPLOSION

Humans domesticated dogs and cats centuries ago. Taken out of their natural environments, dog and cat populations are no longer kept in balance by predators or food limits. Left to their own devices, cats and dogs produce a lot of kittens and puppies. In two years, two cats and their offspring can produce thousands of animals. A fertile dog and its offspring can give birth to 4,372 puppies in seven years. At those rates, it isn't surprising we have problems of overpopulation and homelessness among cats and dogs. Those problems can easily be solved by spaying and neutering.

➤ Every year, nearly 21 million dogs and cats are born in the U.S. About 15 million of those animals are unwanted and end up in shelters or the pound. Those that aren't adopted, 8 to 10 million of them, are put to death.

➤ Excess numbers of animals sometimes elicit cruel behavior from people. Litters of cats are often drowned, and dogs are abandoned. Owners like to think abandoned dogs or cats will fend for themselves, like wild animals, or be taken in by someone who loves strays. In fact, these domesticated, homeless animals usually meet their deaths by starvation, freezing, auto accident, disease, or cruel torture by those who take advantage of their helplessness.

➤ In some states, unwanted animals are given or sold to laboratories, where they become unwilling participants in painful experiments. Every year, hundreds of thousands of lost or abandoned pets go to universities and laboratories for practice surgery, experiments, and testing.

DOG AND CAT RUSTLING

In spite of the rampant overpopulation of dogs and cats, unscrupulous dealers sometimes steal companion animals and sell them to medical schools and researchers.

Unprotected dogs and cats are especially targeted for laboratories that want healthy, people-oriented specimens for laboratory use.

WHAT YOU CAN DO

Adopt a dog or cat from a pound or shelter

Instead of buying a dog or cat from a pet shop, adopt one from a city pound or private animal shelter. Not only will you be boycotting puppy mills, but you may be saving a loving companion animal from being put to death.

If you want a purebred dog (do you really need one?), be sure you visit the breeders and inspect their grounds. Find out if they've taken loving care of their dogs and given them plenty of human contact and room to run. Meet the dog's parents, and be sure you like them. Good breeders who take pride in their dogs, by the way, seldom sell them to pet shops.

Get your dog or cat "fixed"

With animal overpopulation so high, the only responsible course for those who live with cats and/or dogs is to spay or neuter their animals to keep them from reproducing. Spaying and neutering are usually very inexpensive procedures—much cheaper than feeding and caring for new kittens or puppies. And in addition to keeping down the number of homeless, unwanted animals, these procedures can benefit your companion animal.

➤ Spaying a female dog dramatically decreases her chances of mammary cancer and eliminates infections of the uterus and ovaries.

➤ Neutering a male dog reduces his chances of prostate and testicle diseases.

➤ Many male dogs and cats are much friendlier after being neutered. Male dogs that aren't neutered want to roam more (putting them at risk of getting hit by cars) and get into more fights than neutered dogs. Unneutered male cats also fight more and frequently receive bite wounds, which can cause debilitating infections.

➤ Many humane societies, and even some cities, provide low-cost spaying and neutering services or discount coupons. For information on low-cost spay-neuter clinics in your area, call Friends of Animals toll-free at 1-800-631-2212, or call Focus on Animals at 1-800-248-SPAY or 203-377-1116.

Take good care

We're not going to tell you how to take care of your dog or cat—there are plenty of other books on the market that do that. But here are some tips for protecting your companion animal that you won't find in most "pet" books.

Pets don't need plastic surgery. Contrary to many people's beliefs, dogs that receive cosmetic surgery (cropping their tails or ears) suffer in the process. If you have a breed that is usually cropped or clipped, leave it alone. See how wonderful a poodle, for instance, can look with a natural plumed tail.

Protect your dog from loss or theft by making sure he or she has a license tag. Know where your dog or cat is at all times. You can have an identification number tattooed on your dog or cat for a permanent and reliable means of tracing them if they get lost. Contact your veterinarian or animal shelter to find a tattoo registry in your community.

Never leave your dog alone in a car on a hot summer day, even if you leave the windows cracked. On an 85-degree day, the temperature inside a car, with the windows slightly opened, can reach 102 degrees in 10 minutes, and 120 degrees in 30 minutes. A dog can only withstand those kinds of temperatures for a very short time before suffering severe damage. If your dog is overcome by heat exhaustion, give immediate first aid by spraying him with cool water until his body temperature drops.

Pay attention to diet. Many companion animals are over-weight. They need regular exercise and a nutritious diet, without frequent snacks.

Share quality time. Remember that your companion animal needs some quality time with you to play and be loved. And taking a training course with your companion animal will enhance the depth of understanding and communication in your relationship.

Avoid using flea collars, shampoos, and sprays that contain toxic chemicals. It's easy for animals to overdose on the strong insecticides, which are absorbed into their skin. Laboratory testing for these products also, ironically, kills numerous dogs and cats. It's much safer to groom your companion animal daily with a flea comb and to use herbal shampoos. If you do use a toxic flea preparation and notice any vomiting, trembling, diarrhea, or respiratory problems, wash the product off immediately and call the vet.

Here are some companies that sell nontoxic pet products:

Breeders Equipment Co., P.O. Box 177, Flourtown, PA 19030

The Compassionate Consumer, P.O. Box 27, Jericho, NY 11753

EcoSafe Laboratories, P.O. Box 1177, St. Augustine, FL 32085

My Brother's Keeper, P.O. Box 1769, Richmond, IN 47375

Nature Basics, 97 Main St., Box 190, Lancaster, NH 03584

Petguard, Inc., P.O. Box 728, Orange Park, FL 32073, 904-272-6077, 1-800-874-3221

The Pet Connection, P.O. Box 390711, Mountain View, CA 94039, 415-960-1710

Vegetarian dogs and cats

If you're a vegetarian, you might like your cat or dog to be one, too. Vegetarian animal food is available at some health food stores and from the companies listed below. But be sure you meet all your companion animals' nutritional needs if you feed them vegetarian food. Cats, for instance, require high levels of the amino acid taurine, which is most commonly available in flesh foods but can be given as a nonanimal supplement. Without plenty of taurine, cats can go blind. Be sure to consult your veterinarian before changing your animal's diet.

Here are some sources for vegetarian pet supplies:

Amberwood, Route 1, Box 206, Milner, GA 30257, 404-358-2991

Animalove/The Health Emporium for Animals, 530 East Putnam Ave., Dept. AG, Greenwich, CT 06830, 203-869-9888

Cher Ami, 2 East Ave., Larchmont, NY 10538, 914-833-0594

Nyla Bone Corp., Box 427, Neptune, NJ 07753, 201-988-8400 (for dog bones)

Wow-Bow Distributors, Ltd., 309 Burr Rd., East Northport, NY 11731, 516-499-8572

A few important technicalities

Besides being a good friend to your cat or dog, you're his or her guardian. There are a few technicalities—legal and otherwise—that you need to keep in mind. For more complete information on your legal rights and responsibilities with respect to your dog, read *Dog Law*, a self-help book put out by NOLO Press, 950 Parker St., Berkeley, CA 94710 ($12.95). You can also contact the ASPCA's department of legal services for information on your legal rights to have a pet in your apartment or condominium.

License your dog and even your cat. Even if it seems unlikely that your companion animal will run away, bite someone, get stolen, or be retrieved by an animal control officer, it could happen. When unlicensed dogs are found roaming by an animal control officer, they're often euthanized at the pound unless they are wearing a tag. If you want your companion animal returned quickly, you'd better make sure your dog (and in some towns, your cat) is wearing a license tag. If your dog is lost and is not wearing a license tag, call your city pound or animal shelter at once.

Check with your local health department to find out how many dogs or cats you're allowed to keep according to your town's law. If you're over the limit, you may be fined.

Consider health insurance. Health insurance might sound a little extravagant for animals—until you start looking at some big veterinary bills. An operation to excise a tumor, for example, can cost up to $1,000. A good reason to get health insurance is so that you won't be forced to place a dollar value on your companion animal's health. You'll be assured of good care, even if it's expensive. Two companies offer animal health insurance: Animal Health Insurance Agency (1-800-345-6778) and Veterinary Pet Insurance (1-800-USA-PETS).

Provide for your pet in case of your death. You can't leave your money to a cat, but you can ensure that your beloved companion animal will be provided for by naming a caretaker. You can leave your money to that person, along with the request that it be used for the animal's care. If you can't find a friend or relative you can trust, you might ask a charitable organization to adopt your companion animal, or place him in a good home. Be sure to leave that organization enough money to make your animal comfortable for the rest of his life. Your will should also state that your companion animal may not be used for medical research or product testing under any circumstances.

Providing for your dog or cat in your will is as simple as

★ **SUCCESS STORIES** ★

★ Animal activists created enough publicity about conditions in puppy mills in Kansas (where there are about 2,400 such establishments) to convince state legislators to respond. They enacted a law in 1988 requiring registration and semiannual inspections of all commercial breeders and kennels to ensure that dogs used for breeding are given proper shelter, food, and veterinary care.

★ Eleven states have banned the use of shelter animals in laboratory experiments. The World Health Organization and the National Institutes of Health also have recommended against using shelter animals in research.

★ In 1988, the ASPCA handled 16,355 animal cruelty cases, issuing 2,820 citations, and convicting 339 people, many on multiple counts.

★ It's now against the law in Sweden to crop a dog's tail for cosmetic reasons.

including a provision such as "If my cat, Piper, is alive at my death, I leave her and $5,000 for her care to my friend Felix Freedman. If Felix is unable to care for Piper, I leave her and the $5,000 for her care to Priscilla Peters." For more information, read NOLO's *Dog Law* (mentioned above) or call the ASPCA or the Humane Society of the United States (HSUS).

BE A WATCHDOG FOR ANIMAL CRUELTY

It pains us all to see animals who have been neglected or abandoned, chained up in miserable weather, or left without enough food and water. Even when the dog is on the other side of a neighbor's fence, it's important to intervene when you suspect cruelty.

When you suspect cruelty

Try talking to the owner of the mistreated animal. It may be that a little education is all he or she needs to give a dog or cat proper care. If the owner won't take your advice, call your local SPCA or humane society. These agencies monitor the treatment of animals and investigate complaints. Sometimes they work with local law enforcement agencies to look into animal mistreatment. If you don't have a humane society, call a local dog owners' organization, the animal control authorities, or the police or sheriff.

Sometimes direct action may be needed to save a dog or cat's life. If you find a mistreated, hungry stray on the street, try giving her a little food and water. Then call the humane society or—if the dog or cat isn't too scared to be approached—take her there (or home) yourself.

FOR MORE INFORMATION

American Society for the Prevention of Cruelty to Animals (ASPCA). "Puppy Mills," information sheet; *Traveling with Your Pet* (book); *Good Owner, Great Dog* (video), by pet expert Brian Kilcommons.

Animal Legal Defense Fund (ALDF). *Animals' Advocate* (newsletter), Summer 1989: "When You Suspect Veterinary Malpractice" and "Protecting Your Companion Animal."

Focus on Animals. "Throwaways" (video), about spaying and neutering.

The Humane Society of the United States (HSUS). *Are You Getting Your Puppy's Worth?* (pamphlet).

In Defense of Animals. *The Case Against Pound Seizure* (pamphlet).

People for the Ethical Treatment of Animals (PETA). *What Pet Shops Don't Want You to Know* (pamphlet) and factsheets on companion animals.

chapter five

Teach your children well

TEACH YOUR
CHILDREN WELL

Children are always the only future the world has.
—William Saroyan

O ur best hope for a more humane future is to instill humane values in our children. Like any other ethic, respect for animals is learned, not inborn.

We like to think of children as having a natural affinity for animals, an innate trust and kindness for all living things. In reality, children have complex feelings about animals, including fear, and the potential to be cruel. Children need guidance and supervision in relating to animals. Adults have both the opportunity and the responsibility to teach our children to love and respect the animals who share our planet.

We start sending our kids conflicting messages about animals at an early age. With one hand we give them cute and cuddly stuffed animals to sleep with at night; with the other we serve them animals as meals. And while grown-ups use the word "meat" instead of "dead animals" to describe their dinner, eventually the day comes when every kid understands that his hot dog was once a living creature. That may be his or her first philosophical dilemma: Why are we eating the animals we love?

Other confusing messages about animals come at kids from books, television, and movies. Through animated, humanlike characters, children are presented with a bewildering array of "good" animals and "bad" animals. Wolves, rats, and crocodiles are usually portrayed as vicious and cruel. But the "good" animals—lambs, deer, rabbits, and other smiling creatures—don't bear much relation to real animals, either. It's hard for a child to understand, much less revere, the animal kingdom when exposed to these kinds of hero and villain stereotypes. Children need to learn to respect all animals, whether predator or prey, whether wild animals who prefer to be left alone or domesticated animals who depend on our love, kindness, and care.

Meanwhile, our educational system often desensitizes children toward animals. From textbooks that assume meat-eating as the norm to nature projects that call for collecting butterflies and putting pins through these beautiful creatures, to biology labs that promote animal dissection and teach children to kill animals unemotionally in the name of "science"—children learn again and again the cheap price of animal life in our society.

It's often said that today's children will be running tomorrow's world. Only if we become actively involved in their humane education, both through instruction and by example, can we expect our children to create a more compassionate society in the twenty-first century.

RAISING HUMANE CHILDREN

Big Bird and the Big Bad Wolf

When you help your child decide what books to read and what TV shows to watch, choose ones that encourage empathy for animals. Some fairy tales portray animals as villains (like the ubiquitous bad wolf), and others put them in cruel situations (like the Three Blind Mice, who get their tails cut off with a carving knife). If your child reads these tales, it might be a good opportunity to talk about how people have learned to be more respectful of animals.

Many books about farms, and songs like "Old Mac-Donald Had a Farm," present the view that farm animals are happy and contribute to the illusion that they aren't raised to be killed. Most country farms have given way to large-scale, mass-production factory farms.

Fortunately, books and TV shows do exist that are more respectful of animal life. "Sesame Street," "Mister Rogers' Neighborhood," and "Captain Kangaroo" all present very caring, wondrous views of animals. Captain Kangaroo's motto is "Some of my best friends are animals," and he demonstrates what good care he takes of animals throughout the show.

Many children's books convey compassionate attitudes toward animals, including *The Velveteen Rabbit* and *Bambi*. New pro-animal books for kids include *Animal Rights* by Patricia Curtis, *The Magic Finger* by Roald Dahl, and *Much Ado about Aldo* by Johanna Hurwitz. There's a list of other humane books for children at the end of this chapter.

➤ *Otterwise* is a publication "for kids who love animals," available for $4 a year at P.O. Box 1374, Portland, ME 04104.

➤ *Kind News* and *Children & Animals* are pro-animal publications with lots of ideas for children, available for $20 a year from the National Association for the Advancement of Humane and Environmental Education, P.O. Box 362, East Haddam, CT 06423.

➤ People for the Ethical Treatment of Animals puts out a quarterly publication, *PETA Kids*, with articles, games, and suggestions for children. Available for $2 a year from PETA, P.O. Box 42516, Washington, DC 20015-0516.

➤ The American Society for the Prevention of Cruelty to Animals puts out *Children's Pages*, which features information and activities for children who want to help protect animals. For a free copy of the latest edition, write to the ASPCA at 441 East 92nd St., New York, N.Y. 10128.

Terrible toy tests

Like cosmetic and household products, toys are often needlessly tested on animals to determine their safety. To test toy guns, manufacturers point the guns in animals' faces and see if the plastic pieces discharged hurt the animal.

ANIMAL AWARENESS

Spend an hour some Saturday morning watching cartoons with your child. Choose one of the dozen television shows that feature anthropomorphized animals. Talk to your child about how the animals are portrayed and what situations they're put in. Are the animals treated violently? What happens when a real animal gets hit on the head? Are some of the cartoon animals always mean and others always nice?

Next, take your child to the library and find a book about one of the animals featured in a cartoon. A real, non-Ninja turtle, for instance. Or a pig other than Porky—one that moves about on four legs, not two, and doesn't talk. Read the book together and talk about the differences between real animals and cartoon characters.

That afternoon, go on a field trip in search of the animal in the book. You might look in a park, a nature center, or a small family farm. Binoculars are good for close-up views of wild animals. Take along some paper and pens to draw pictures of what real animals look like and how they live. How about bringing along a vegetarian picnic for two?

Substances like modeling clay are force-fed to animals to test toxicity. Other tests involve dropping toys on animals to see if any protruding parts hurt them. Not only are these tests cruel, they're unnecessary. Most toy companies have new, high-tech methods of testing their toys for safety—without harming animals.

Boycott toy companies that test on animals. You and your child can help put a stop to these tests by writing to the companies that still use them. For an up-to-date and complete list of companies that don't test on animals (including Hasbro, Kenner, Mattel, Worlds of Wonder), as well as those that do, contact PETA at 301-770-7444.

Vegi-kids

The simplest way to instill respect for animal life in a child is to offer them vegetarian meals. Vegetarian children are spared the conflicting message that we should love animals but eat them, too.

You may worry that a vegetarian diet might not provide enough nutrition for your child. But studies have shown that vegetarian children surpass meat-eating children in dietary excellence. Researchers at the University of Nebraska compared the body measurements and nutrition of ovo-lacto-vegetarian kids aged 10 to 12 to those of their omnivorous peers. The vegetarian boys and girls ate less fat, cholesterol, and protein and more carbohydrates than the meat-eaters—putting them right in line with dietary recommendations to reduce heart disease and overweight.

With a little care, you can raise a very healthy vegetarian child. Millions of children around the world are vegetarians—and thriving. With obesity becoming more and more of a children's problem, feeding them a diet with lots of vegetables and grains, and less fat, makes good sense. Degenerative diseases caused by too much fat and excess protein start in childhood. Scientists have found atherosclerosis in its beginning stages in infants of nine months.

Check to see if there are vegetarian alternatives for lunch at your child's school. If not, work with the cafeteria manager, the school board, or the P.T.A. to provide them.

Here are some helpful resources for vegetarian parents:

➤ *The Complete Guide and Cookbook to Raising Your Child as a Vegetarian.* Michael and Nina Shandler. Schocken, 1981.

➤ *The Vegetarian Child.* Joy Gross. Lyle Stewart Publishers, 1983.

➤ *Vegetarian Baby* and *Vegetarian Children.* Sharon Yntema. Available from *Vegetarian Times,* 1-800-435-0715.

➤ Companies making baby products that aren't tested on animals include Autumn Harp, Aubrey Organics, Country Comfort, Creature Care, and Mild and Natural.

ANIMALS WEREN'T CREATED TO ENTERTAIN

Take a hard look at zoos

Going to the zoo might seem like a natural way to teach children about animals. But what do most zoos really teach? You won't observe animals in their natural habitats, behaving as they normally would. Instead, children will probably watch large captive animals pacing back and forth in small pens or other bored animals listlessly lying in their cages. The best modern zoos have reputable research programs that encourage endangered species preservation. But antiquated zoos and most roadside menageries teach a sad lesson in the human subjugation of animals.

➤ How do animals get to the zoo? You might imagine that most zoo tenants are abandoned wild animals who were rescued and placed in a zoo to insure their survival. In fact, many healthy animals are snatched out of their natural habitats and brutally transferred to a cage, where they're prevented from following their most basic instincts, such as gathering food. In order to capture baby chimpanzees, poachers usually shoot the mother and kidnap the child. And only 1 in 10 baby chimps survives the journey to the zoo.

➤ Zoos can miseducate children about wild animals. Animals pacing, circling, weaving, and compulsively licking and grooming themselves teach children less about healthy wildlife than about the symptoms of confinement.

➤ Are zoos necessary to protect endangered species?

Unfortunately and increasingly, yes. But captive breeding (which is often not successful) is no solution to the global destruction of species. Only habitat protection can slow the current massive extinction of species, and the idea that zoos can replace natural habitats risks further endangering our wild species. Unless we quickly take steps to better protect our wild habitats, zoos may be the only places in which more and more animals species can survive.

➤ Besides being bored, zoo animals often suffer mistreatment. They lack privacy and cannot live according to their natural needs. Aquatic animals have very little water, animals who usually live in herds are forced to live alone, and animals of all types are prevented from stalking, natural mating, flying, running, climbing, and other instinctive behaviors.

➤ Animals bred in zoos may be sold to laboratories for experiments, or to circuses, where their fate may be worse than in zoos. Some zoo animals end up in "wild game" parks or hunting preserves, where people pay thousands of dollars to shoot an ailing lion or tiger at point-blank range.

If you do take your children to a zoo, or if they go there on a school field trip, have them make a list of the good and bad things they see there. You might suggest that they write a letter to the zoo director about specific problems they may have witnessed.

Children can better learn about animals by studying them in their natural environments. Community nature centers, wildlife refuges, and parks are good places to study wildlife without disturbing it.

Boycott the Big Top

To children, the circus is a fantastic spectacle of glitter, lights, magic, and animals with amazing talents. But they don't realize that circuses may also be one of the greatest examples of people's cruelty to animals. Not only are circus animals taken out of their natural habitats, they are confined in cramped cages. Sometimes they have inadequate food and drinking water; often a veterinarian is nowhere to be found. When it comes time to be trained, they endure tight collars and muzzles and are whipped and prodded to perform senseless tricks for the sake of entertainment.

➤ Some circus animals are drugged to make them more obedient, while others have their teeth and claws removed.

➤ When circus animals have outlived their usefulness, they are often sold to zoos, private collectors, game farms, or research laboratories.

You don't have to go to an animal circus to treat kids to the magic of the big top. Some circuses and acrobatic performances don't use any animals at all but are nevertheless wonderful to watch, such as the Cirque de Soleil from Canada and the Pickle Family Circus from San Francisco.

Say whoa to rodeo

Rodeos are more a demonstration of people's domination over animals than their skill in riding or roping. Rather than wild, untamed range animals, the horses, calves, bulls, and steer used in rodeo are show animals that spend a lifetime of stress being transported from one rodeo to another. They are captive performers, housed in cramped trailers and pens, then whipped into a frenzy for the sake of a show.

➤ Bucking broncos aren't wild horses that need to be broken. They've simply been strapped so tightly around their tender flanks that they are wild to rid themselves of the pain. Electric prods, sticks, painful ointments, and other devices are used to enrage the animals and keep them in line.

➤ In the calf-roping event, calves running nearly 30 miles an hour are lassoed around the neck and dragged to the ground. The result is often severe bruising, neck and back injuries, internal hemorrhaging, and broken bones.

➤ Steer busting, in which the steer is lassoed and knocked

to the ground, often busts horns and bones, and the steer is usually stunned and knocked unconscious.

➤ Many rodeos don't even offer veterinary care to animals, who often suffer open wounds, skin infections, cracked hooves, and other maladies.

4-H and the Boy Scouts

➤ With nearly 4 million members, the 4-H Club is the country's largest organization for youths. Like Future Farmers of America, 4-H is heavily subsidized by the meat and dairy industries—and it's no mystery why. The main activity of 4-H Club members is to raise, groom, and show animals—and then sell them to the slaughterhouse. Children often go through a lot of emotional pain when the animal they lovingly cared for ends up on the butcher block.

If you want to instill young people with compassion and respect for animals, consider volunteering as a scout leader. You might be surprised at the interest you can generate by cooking a vegetarian meal around a campfire. Though kindness is part of scout law, Boy Scouts haven't always lived up to their code when it comes to animals. Some outings have included "survival skills" like rabbit hunting (wouldn't finding edible plants be easier?) as well as "pest control" contests to kill the most birds, coyotes, raccoons, gophers, and skunks. If you want to take an active, positive role in scouting, write to: Ben Love, Chief Scout Executive, Boy Scouts of America, 1325 Walnut Hill Lane, Irving, TX 75015.

BE SURE THINGS ARE COOL AT SCHOOL

As parents, we're responsible for our children's education. What does your child's school teach about animals?

Some educational experiences are positive, such as watching films of animals in nature and learning the roles of various animals (including humans) in the ecological chain.

But anti-animal sentiments often creep into lessons. For example, many textbooks have spelling exercises with sentences like "Lamb is my favorite meat." The assumption that humans must kill animals and eat meat is rarely questioned. Other lessons ask students to list all the ways animals can be "used." Correct answers include "for fur, food, hunting, and experimental research."

Some classrooms keep animals, such as gerbils, birds, hamsters, guinea pigs, and rabbits. But what do children really learn by keeping animals in cages?

Children are desensitized to animal life in other ways at school. Students are instructed to mount insect collections with pins. Science experiments often use chicken embryos or other animals. And the dissection of animals may start as early as elementary school.

Talk to the teacher and, if necessary, the principal or school board members if your child's elementary school class uses texts or projects that promote the killing of animals.

Take a "field trip" to a real field. Have the students study insects and animals in their natural environments—without harming them.

If your school sends children on field trips to zoos, petting zoos, aquariums, country fairs, farms, or circuses, let the teacher know why you would prefer your child not participate. Suggest alternatives, such as nature hikes. If your child does go on the field trip, talk with him about what he saw and about how animals were treated there.

Go to P.T.A. meetings and raise the issue of humane education with teachers and other parents. Point out ways in which children are being taught inhumane lessons at school and suggest that the group propose improvements to the principal or school board.

A wide range of teaching materials is available for humane education. Here are a few we found:

Educators' Newsletter. Focus on Animals, P.O. Box 150, Trumbull, CT 06611.

Humane Education Manual. ASPCA.

Humane Education: A Teacher's Guide. Los Angeles Society for the Prevention of Cruelty to Animals, 5026 West Jefferson Blvd., Los Angeles, CA 90016.

Humane Education Committee, P.O. Box 445, Gracie Station, New York, NY 10028.

Kind News and *Children & Animals.* National Association for the Advancement of Humane and Environmental Education, P.O. Box 362, East Haddam, CT 06423.

Respect them, don't dissect them

Most secondary (and some elementary) students in the United States are expected to participate in animal dissection as part of their biology classes. Dissecting frogs, fetal pigs, chipmunks, mice, and other animals is not only repulsive to many students, but it desensitizes them to animal life. The study of a "life science," which is meant to instill curiosity and respect for life, becomes the study of needless death.

Every year, over 6.7 million animals are killed to be dissected for educational experiments in the U.S. Many of these animals are collected from their natural environments; in the process, their habitats may be threatened. Other animals, including mice, rabbits, and pigs, are bred in cramped "factories" solely for the purpose of being sold later for experiments.

Check out the alternatives

There are numerous educational alternatives to dissection, ranging from detailed models and computer simulations to films of animals in their natural habitat.

Recently, high school students have started to speak out against dissection. With the help of their parents, they are raising the awareness of the school and community and creating an educational environment where animals' lives are respected, not dissected.

Students can best refuse to dissect by letting the teacher know early on in the course about their objections, so that alternative assignments can be developed.

★ SUCCESS STORIES ★

★ California recently passed a law giving students (kindergarten through high school) the right to refuse to dissect, harm, or kill animals—and the right to substitute an alternative project. Teachers must inform students of their right to not participate in dissection assignments, and students cannot be penalized for refusing to dissect.

★ The National Science Teachers Association (NSTA) and the National Association of Biology Teachers (NABT) have come out with published guidelines discouraging harmful experiments on live vertebrates. The guidelines are available from NSTA, 1742 Connecticut Ave., NW, Washington, DC 20009.

★ The latest edition of *Modern Biology* (Holt, Rinehart and Winston, 1988), one of the most popular high school biology textbooks, does not include dissections of animals because "for most students behavioral observations foster a greater respect for living organisms."

★ Animal rights advocates, including many children, helped change the policies of Tonka Toys (which also owns Kenner) from testing on animals to making cruelty-free products.

★ In September 1988 schoolchildren marched on City Hall in New York City to demand funding for humane education programming in every classroom within the N.Y.C. Public School System.

Here are some humane alternatives you or your child can suggest:

➤ *The Anatomy Coloring Book*, by Wynn Kapit and Lawrence M. Elson (Harper & Row, 1977), is an excellent resource for teaching students about anatomy and physiology.

➤ "Operation Frog" is a computer software program that simulates the dissection and reconstruction of the frog, using proper sequence and instruments. Available from Scholastic Software, Inc., P.O. Box 7502, 2931 East McCarty St., Jefferson City, MO 65102.

➤ "Alternative Project Sheets" is a collection of specific alternatives to some of the most common animal-related biology experiments and dissections. Available from the National Association for the Advancement of Humane Education, P.O. Box 362, East Haddam, CT 06423.

➤ Many other models, videotapes, books, and projects are available as alternatives to dissection. For more information, write to the Animal Legal Defense Fund, 1363 Lincoln Ave., San Rafael, CA 94901. Or call their Dissection Hotline, 1-800-922-FROG.

The Animal Legal Defense Fund and the ASPCA also give legal support to students who refuse to dissect animals. An ASPCA video on laboratory research issues, "A Question of Respect," is available for $69.95 through Varied Directions, 1-800-888-5236.

HUMANE CHILDREN'S BOOKS

The Gnats of Knotty Pine. Bill Peet. Houghton Mifflin, 1975.

Where Can the Animals Go? Ron Wegen. Greenwillow, 1978.

Oh, No, Cat! Janice May Udry. Coward, McCann & Geoghegan, 1976.

Mousekin's Golden House. Edna Miller. Prentice-Hall, 1964.

The Rabbits' Wedding. Garth Williams. Harper & Row, 1958.

The Winter Cat. Howard Knotts. Harper & Row, 1972.

The Mice Came In Early This Year. Eleanor Lapp. Albert Whitman, 1976.

Go Away, Dog. Joan Nodset. Harper & Row, 1963.

The Happy Day. Ruth Krauss. Harper & Row, 1949.

Alexander and the Wind-Up Mouse. Leo Lionni. Pantheon, 1969.

FOR MORE INFORMATION

American Society for the Prevention of Cruelty to Animals (ASPCA). "Learning to Care," in *ASPCA Report* (newletter), vol. 8, no. 2.

Animal Legal Defense Fund. Dissection Hotline: 1-800-922-FROG. *Students Against Dissection* (brochure).

The Animals' Voice (magazine), vol. 2, no. 2.

Freeman, Barbara. *Animals, Kids and Books* (booklet). Available from 431 Ferrell Drive, Fayetteville, NC 28303, for $3.

Jamieson, Dale. "Against Zoos," in *In Defense of Animals*, ed. Peter Singer. Harper & Row, 1985.

People for the Ethical Treatment of Animals (PETA). *Toy Companies and Animal Testing* and *Rodeo: Cruelty for a Buck* (factsheets).

chapter six

LET WILDLIFE LIVE

LET WILDLIFE LIVE

*We are part of the earth and it is part of us. The
perfumed flowers are our sisters; the deer, the horse,
the great eagle: these are our brothers. All things are
connected like the blood which unites one's family.*

— Chief Seattle

I
n the time it takes you to read this chapter, an entire
species will vanish from the face of our planet. It will
probably be a species that humans never encountered,
much less identified or named.

Humankind will extinguish between half a million
and 2 million species—15 to 20 per cent of all species on
earth—by the year 2000. In what amounts to the geologic
blink of an eye, we are now killing off more species of plants
and animals than all those that disappeared during the last
ice age.

The extermination of nonhuman species is animal
cruelty carried to its logical and most frightening conclusion. Armed with the weapons of modern industry and
technology, the urge to subjugate animals has been fully
realized in our life and death control over all of the Earth's
creatures. We humans have finally proven that we are
indeed superior to other animals.

Or have we? In our arrogance, we have failed to take
note of one very obvious fact: Our own survival is intimately
tied to the fate of the animal kingdom and the planet we are
so busily destroying. Our civilization's urge to subjugate
every living thing, it turns out, is suicidal.

Today, we are learning this lesson in a hurry. Entire
ecosystems are collapsing, thanks to our voracious appetite
for developing wild land, exploiting natural resources, and
killing animals for sport. Toxic substances meant to control
"pests" in farming are returning to pollute our groundwater

and sicken our children. Destruction of the rainforest and its plant and animal inhabitants is undermining our planet's ability to regulate the climate and clean the atmosphere—and is robbing us of potential life-saving medicines.

People, wilderness, and wildlife are all integral parts of one fragile biosphere, which is teetering in a complex balancing act of interdependence. This balance is maintained by diversity—when one species disappears *gradually*, another may take its place over time, reweaving itself into the web of life. But when we threaten thousands of species simultaneously, the balance of nature becomes more and more precarious for us all.

A MATTER OF HABITAT

It all comes down to this: Wild animals need wilderness to survive. They cannot live in areas that humans have significantly altered. When people destroy any unique habitat, whether it's wetland or rainforest, it results in the suffering and eventual death—and often, extinction—of that land's wild animals.

Wildlife are under siege all over the world; their space to eat, roam, and breed is being rapidly and drastically reduced. Rainforests, home to millions of species—many not yet discovered—are being cut and burned on a massive scale. Wetlands that serve as breeding grounds for birds are being filled in and built over. Forests that are home to deer, owls, and bears are being clear-cut like there's no tomorrow. Lakes, rivers, harbors, and oceans are collapsing under the sheer weight of human interference and pollution.

Unless we take immediate measures to protect the integrity of wildlife environments, the mad dash to species extinction will continue unchecked.

Problems on the prairie

In much of the western United States, the prairie has given way to large-scale cattle ranching and lamb farming.

ANIMAL AWARENESS

Wildlife doesn't always come with spots or stripes and live in Africa. Wherever *you* live, wild animals once lived and probably still do. So instead of going to the zoo, pay a visit to your real, local wildlife. If you live in a city (even one populated by millions of people), there's bound to be wild habitat like parks, marshes, lagoons, estuaries, and creeks where various birds, fish, reptiles, raccoons, squirrels, and even deer may live.

If you love having companion animals in your home, you're sure to enjoy finding out about your wildlife neighbors. These native animals counteract the artificial feel of many cities; their vigor indicates how healthy the local ecosystem is; and their behaviors—such as migrations, rutting, and bearing young—teach us about nature and the changing seasons. Buy a topographic map of your town or city and identify all the likely places, usually near water, where wildlife might live. Then go pay them a visit. Or call your local nature center or environmental group to find out when the next hike or nature walk is scheduled.

The coyotes that used to roam freely on the land are now often shot by ranchers. When these predators disappear from the food chain, raccoons, squirrels, and crows have no natural enemies. In their unchecked proliferation, they wipe out many of the lovely songbirds that migrate across the plains.

➤ Native populations of wolves in the lower 48 states have been virtually wiped out by habitat destruction, shootings, and government-sponsored "predator control" programs.

➤ There are now 95% fewer songbirds flying in the Midwest than there were 100 years ago. Songbird loss is a result of pesticide use, habitat destruction, and nesting competition from introduced species such as sparrows and starlings.

Deserted deserts

The desert is perhaps the Earth's most fragile and misunderstood ecosystem. Because it doesn't flaunt its secrets, people assume there's little or no wildlife there. But the desert is home to many creatures: lizards, toads, rats, roadrunners, coyotes, bighorn sheep, squirrels, eagles, and quail. The California desert, for example, has over 2,500 plant and animal species. But desert habitats are now threatened by commercial development, nuclear waste storage, and recreational use of off-road vehicles.

➤ A single motorcycle displaces about three-quarters of a ton of fragile desert soil per mile. The lost soil reduces plant life needed by all desert animals to survive, with devastating results.

➤ Tortoises, many of which are endangered, are starving to death in the Mojave Desert as a direct result of off-road vehicles ripping up their food sources. In the desert's arid environment, this damage takes thousands of years to recover.

Don't use off-road vehicles in the desert, and vote for legislation that restricts or removes these vehicles.

Tropical topics

Fully half of all the species in the world inhabit the densely populated tropics, the 3.4-million-square-mile green band that encircles the equator in Africa, South and Central America, and Asia. Here is where the problem of habitat destruction is at its worst.

Tropical rainforests are being destroyed at an alarming rate, the victims of logging, cattle ranching, and farming. Already half the Earth's rainforests have been burned, cut, and bulldozed. And when those lush habitats are clear-cut or burned, thousands of animals perish. Studies estimate that tropical deforestation wipes out 17,000 species of plants and animals per year.

➤ A four-mile patch of rainforest usually contains up to 125 different species of mammals, 400 kinds of birds, 100 reptiles, 60 amphibians, and innumerable insects. Considering that 74,000 acres of rainforest are destroyed per day, the toll of animal life is immense and immeasurable.

➤ South and Central American rainforests are cleared primarily to establish grazing lands for beef cattle to meet the growing demands of the world's hamburger stands. Ironically, rainforest land makes very poor pasture, because most of the nutrients are in the tropical growth, not in the soil. After two years of cattle grazing the soil is depleted, and the ranchers have to burn new rainforests for new cattle land.

➤ One out of three bird species found in the world nests in the rainforest, some 2,600 species in all. A single wildlife reserve in Costa Rica is home to more bird species than the entire North American continent.

➤ Many rainforest animals face extinction. One example is the jaguar, which requires vast expanses of untrammeled jungle to hunt and roam. Future generations may only know a jaguar as a type of car.

➤ Exotic birds and other animals are hunted down to be sold as pets. Many beautiful and rare birds, like those from the parrot family, are becoming endangered because of capture and resale in the U.S. After being snagged in the jungle, the birds are transported under cruel conditions, often crammed into tiny boxes where they endure heat, thirst, hunger, and disease. Only one in five survives.

➤ Some experts estimate that two species are lost every hour due to rainforest destruction.

Avoid eating beef. Rainforests in the tropics are being burned to make way for cattle farms. The animals in those forests are burned, too, or die when they have nowhere to go and nothing to eat.

Don't buy furniture and lumber made from tropical hardwoods.

Write to the Rainforest Action Network, 301 Broadway, Suite A, San Francisco, CA 94133, or call 415-398-4404, to find out what you can do to help save the rainforests and tropics.

Buy a copy of *The Rainforest Book: How You Can Save the World's Rainforests* (Living Planet Press, 1990, $5.95) or send $5.95 plus $2 shipping to NRDC, P.O. Box 1400, Church Hill, MD 21690.

The Arctic and other climes

The problem of disappearing habitat—and species—isn't limited to a few corners of the world. Almost everywhere you can imagine, animals are threatened.

➤ The Arctic National Wildlife Refuge in northeastern Alaska—America's largest remaining wilderness—is threatened by proposed oil exploration in the Beaufort Sea coastal plain. This plain is the calving ground of Alaska's plentiful Porcupine caribou, and is also home to polar bears, wolverines, and musk oxen.

➤ Mountain lions, which were abundant in North America 80 years ago, are now nearly extinct. Poisoned, hunted, and trapped in the past, the principal threat to the remaining thousands is habitat loss. Many myths surround the mountain lion: that they are a major cause of livestock loss and a threat to public safety, and that their numbers are growing. It is true that there have been increased sightings of mountain lions—because of the ever-encroaching development of wild lands, they simply have fewer places to hide.

➤ Grizzly bears, which once roamed the West in great numbers, have dwindled to fewer than 1,000 in the lower 48 states. Even their few remaining habitats are now threatened as the Forest Service invites logging, mining, drilling, and clear-cutting into the bears' last homes. The California grizzly bear became extinct in 1922; we will have to act now to save remaining grizzlies.

➤ In Australia, the koala bear, once prolific, now faces the possibility of extinction. This beautiful animal needs a lot of space to roam. Development has wiped out nearly 80% of its habitat.

African wildlife

The majestic, lumbering elephant has been a source of human awe and delight for centuries. But now elephants are facing a two-pronged threat. Not only is their habitat being eliminated, but they are still being hunted for their tusks, despite the trade ban many countries have placed on ivory.

To supply consumer demand for ivory products, poachers track down elephants, shoot or stun them, and tear the tusks from their heads. Often the animal is still alive during the mutilation. After the tusks are removed, the animal is left to die in the blistering heat, either bleeding to death or dying of thirst. Some poachers cut off the elephants' faces with chainsaws to get the tusks.

As the elephant population dwindles, younger and younger elephants are killed. Even baby elephants, with tusks no larger than pencils, are being poached for ivory.

➤ It is estimated that at the current rate of poaching, the African elephant will be extinct within 5 to 10 years.

➤ Flying over Africa, people see more elephant carcasses than living elephants.

➤ As the supply of ivory from African elephants drops because of overhunting, poachers are turning to walruses. Native Americans and Soviet natives kill walruses for food—up to 12,000 a year—but recently poachers have been killing the animals just for their tusks.

Don't buy ivory. It's consumer demand that drives the international trade in ivory—and it is driving the African elephant over the cliff of extinction. Only when consumer demand dries up will the killing stop.

Elephants aren't the only African wildlife in trouble:

➤ 90% of black rhinos have been slaughtered for their horns (favored for use as dagger handles throughout the Middle East).

➤ Rwandan mountain gorillas faced certain extinction before the timely intervention of Diane Fossey (as portrayed by Sigourney Weaver in *Gorillas in the Mist*). Their young continue to be captured and sold to the zoo and menagerie trade, and gorilla heads and paws are still used as "decorative pieces."

Deadly nets

Many commercial fisherman kill more than fish when they cast their big nets in the ocean. Driftnets, used primarily by Japanese fleets, may stretch for miles in a form of aquatic "strip mining." All kinds of marine creatures become tangled in these deadly plastic webs, including dolphins, whales, marine birds, seals, and marine turtles. More than 1,500 ships in the Pacific Ocean cast over 30,000 miles of net each night during the fishing season.

➤ 30,000 northern fur seals die each year from entanglement in fishing lines, abandoned nets, and six-pack rings.

➤ Torn nets are usually thrown overboard. These "phantom nets" can continue to drift and kill marine life for months.

➤ 6.5 million dolphins have been killed by tuna fishermen who use purse seine nets. These circular nets are often set around schools of dolphins to catch the tuna who swim below them. When the nets are drawn closed (like a drawstring purse) the dolphins are caught and drowned along with the tuna. Bowing to a consumer boycott, major tuna processors recently pledged not to buy or sell tuna caught in these kinds of nets.

For information about protecting dolphins, contact the ASPCA, the Fund for Animals, the Animal Welfare Institute, the Marine Mammal Fund (MMF), HSUS, or Earth Island Institute. "Where Have All the Dolphins Gone?", a video produced by the ASPCA and MMF, is available through the MMF at Fort Mason Center, San Francisco, CA 94123.

Save the whales

Whales face many environmental threats, but they are primarily depleted by fishermen who hunt them. Much whaling can be attributed to Japanese whaling vessels. Traditionally, they have hunted a species to near extinction, then moved on to others. Currently, they harpoon mostly minke and sperm whales.

Write letters to protest Japanese whaling to The Honorable Ambassador, Embassy of Japan, 2520 Massachusetts Ave., NW, Washington, DC 20008.

Write to Greenpeace, 1436 U St., NW, Washington, DC 20009 for more information.

Plastic and pollution at sea

One of the biggest threats to marine wildlife is plastic that humans discard and toss into the ocean. Marine creatures get entangled, caught, and strangled in plastic.

➤ Of all the garbage picked up during beach clean-ups coordinated by the Center for Marine Conservation, 62% is made of plastic, including bags, bottles, fishing lines, and six-pack holders.

➤ Marine mammals sometimes mistake plastics for food. The plastic can cause internal injury, intestinal blockage, or starvation. Several whales are found dead each year with plastic bags and sheeting in their stomachs.

➤ Thousands of marine animals die each year from being entangled in plastic trash, especially six-pack rings and fishing lines. Some sea birds pick up plastic for nesting material, which creates a menace to their young.

➤ Sea turtles, which are endangered, frequently swallow plastic bags, mistaking them for jellyfish, one of their favorite foods. The turtles' habitats are also threatened by pollution of beaches, which are their nesting areas.

➤ The U.S. Coast Guard estimates that recreational boaters dump an average of 1.5 pounds of garbage per person into the ocean each time they go boating.

➤ Approximately 75 tons of trash per week are left by beach-goers in Los Angeles.

Help clean up beaches, and leave the beach clean after you go. If you're a boater, be sure you and your friends never throw trash overboard.

Use biodegradable or recyclable materials instead of plastic products and packaging whenever possible.

Volunteer to rescue sick sea animals. Volunteers make up 95% of the work force of the California Marine Mammal Center, taking care of sick and injured California sea lions, northern elephant seals, harbor seals, northern fur seals, Stellar sea lions, Guadaloupe fur seals, dolphins, porpoises, gray whales, and killer whales. Call 415-331-0161 for information.

CALL OFF THE HUNT

Why do people hunt?

It's hard to understand why people deliberately kill animals in the name of sport, or how they could derive pleasure from a game of terror and painful death. Last year, some 20 million U.S. hunters shot more than 100 million animals. And for every animal that they killed and claimed, another wounded creature died slowly from bleeding, infection, and starvation.

As taxpayers, you and I subsidize this bloody recreation. Only 10% of the population hunts, yet the rest of us pay for the state and federal wildlife agencies that artificially increase wildlife populations to satisfy hunters. Hunting licenses account for only a fraction of the cost of hunting programs. Overpopulation is an unnatural condition created—by our tax dollars—for the benefit of hunters.

Hunters will argue that they eat the meat and use the skin of the animal they have killed. They'll also tell you that they're doing a service to wildlife by helping to prevent overpopulation and misery.

Here's what you can argue in response:

➤ Humans have evolved to the point that we don't need to cause animal suffering for our clothes or food; we have other alternatives.

➤ Hunting does not prevent wildlife overpopulation. On the contrary, "wildlife management" is a technique used in most hunting areas to insure a "maximum sustained yield" of deer (or other "game"). What it actually means is that natural populations are manipulated to keep them artificially high in order to have more deer to kill when hunting season rolls around.

➤ Techniques of "game management" include killing more males than females to keep the population high, using "controlled burning" and pesticides to create grassy vegetation to feed grazing animals, and planting crops for deer.

Hunters argue that they're helping deer by keeping down the population. Yet most hunters will kill the deers' natural predators, too, which only increases the population problem (if a real one exists). In 1989, hunters killed 30,000 black bears and 1,000 endangered brown and grizzly bears.

➤ Not only hunters, but game and wildlife managers also exterminate natural (and often endangered) predators, like wolves and mountain lions, in order to increase deer populations for unnatural predators—people.

➤ Hunters wound and kill not only the animals they're tracking, but people, too. In 1987, 110 people were killed and 1,500 people were injured in hunting accidents.

➤ Some big-game parks offer hunters a chance to shoot

★ SUCCESS STORIES ★

★ Over 100 countries have signed the Convention on International Trade in Endangered Species of Wild Fauna and Flora (CITES), a treaty that protects endangered species and outlaws their international trade. In 1989, CITES placed the elephant on the list of endangered species and approved a ban on the international trade in ivory.

★ Because of a consumer boycott led by environmental and humane groups, the world's major tuna processors announced in March 1990 that they would refuse to purchase any tuna caught in purse seine nets, which are responsible for the deaths of millions of dolphins.

★ In 1988, it became illegal for any ship to dump its plastic trash in U.S. oceans or navigable waters.

★ Because of the efforts of environmentalists, 11 states have passed laws requiring plastic six-pack carriers to be made with new degradable plastics, so that if they are thrown away or lost they will not pollute our oceans.

★ Animal activists have helped close off the markets for seals. The Canadian government announced a total ban on the commercial killing of whitecoat and blueback seals, and the European Community banned the import of baby seal skins permanently.

★ The wolf, once near extinction, is on the rebound because of environmental efforts. Recovery and reintroduction efforts are underway in the Rocky Mountains, the Southwest, and the northern Midwest.

★ In response to worldwide citizen protests, virtually every country is now observing a moratorium on whale hunting.

exotic animals, like lions and elephants. Often these poor creatures are refugees from circuses or zoos, and hunters shoot them at point-blank range for the pleasure of having their photo taken with their "catch."

➤ Lead shot, used in bird and fowl hunting over water, causes lead poisoning in geese, ducks, and other wildlife that inadvertently ingest lead shot when they feed.

Don't hunt! Antlers look best on their original owners.

Study how your state wildlife agency makes decisions. The Animal Legal Defense Fund (ALDF) has filed suit in Massachusetts to challenge the composition of the State Fisheries and Wildlife Board, made up entirely of hunters, fishers, and trappers, with no representation from animal protection or environmental advocates. To find out how you may be better represented, call ALDF at 415-459-0885.

Work with animal rights groups that oppose hunting. The ASPCA, as part of the Wildlife Refuge Reform Coalition, supports legislation to keep wildlife refuges free from hunters and opposes legislation outlawing conscientious harassment of hunters. Other groups active against hunting include the Fund for Animals, Friends of Animals, Animal Protection Institute, the Humane Society of the United States, and the American Humane Association.

Post "No Hunting" signs if you own land.

Before you join or contribute to wildlife or conservation groups, find out whether they support hunting. Some of the oldest and largest groups were founded by hunters who were primarily interested in preserving wild lands and wild animals for future generations of hunters. Call or write to ask them about their current position on hunting.

A few *more* things you can do for wildlife

Learn to treat wild animals with respect, and teach your children to do the same. If you run across wild animals while hiking, don't try to feed or pet them. Use binoculars if you want a close-up view. Go out of your way to give wildlife some space.

Share a newspaper. The manufacture of newsprint requires toxic chemicals; these end up in the water supplies that animals need to drink.

Use recycled paper. Pulp and paper mills use a lot of chlorine-based bleach, a poison to almost every known animal.

Always vote pro-wilderness when a land-use issue comes up in a local election. If your town is considering filling in a wetlands to build condominiums, vote against it. There are lots of condos, but only a few good wetlands for migratory birds.

Write to your state and national representatives to let them know how important wildlife conservation issues are to you.

Try to buy organically grown fruits and vegetables. The pesticide runoff from treated vegetables pollutes streams and causes the animals who drink from them to become ill.

Donate to The Nature Conservancy, which buys natural lands and preserves them for wildlife: The Nature Conservancy, 1815 North Lynn St., Arlington, VA 22209, 703-841-5300.

FOR MORE INFORMATION

American Society for the Prevention of Cruelty to Animals (ASPCA). "The Price *They* Pay," video on fur, ivory, and wildlife exploitation.

Animal Welfare Institute, "The Noble Elephant" (brochure).

Animal Protection Institute of America. "Endangered Species" (brochure).

Center for Marine Conservation. "Facts and Figures on Marine Debris" (booklet).

Defenders of Wildlife. *Defenders* (magazine).

Greenpeace. "Sea Turtles" and "Japanese Whaling" (Greenpeace action sheets).

International Wildlife Coalition, "Ivory: Poaching Elephants to Extinction for Their Tusks" (brochure).

People for the Ethical Treatment of Animals (PETA). Factsheets on hunting, especially "Hunting: Unfair Game."

Planet Drum Books. *A Green City Program.* P.O. Box 31251, San Francisco, CA 94131.

Progressive Animal Welfare Society (PAWS). "Dolphins in Peril," in *PAWS News*, April 1990.

Wildlife Refuge Reform Coalition, P.O. Box 18414, Washington, DC 20036.

chapter seven

SPEAKING OUT
FOR ANIMAL RIGHTS

SPEAKING OUT
FOR ANIMAL RIGHTS

*The greatness of a nation and its moral progress
can be judged by the way its animals are treated.*

— Mahatma Gandhi

So far, we've told you about many of the simple, everyday ways you can start saving animal lives. These have been mostly personal actions—reexamining choices about what you eat, wear, and buy to help make the world more humane. Personal changes are important, but animals also need humans to *speak out* on their behalf.

You'll have a much greater impact if you tell other people—your neighbors, your newspaper, or your elected representatives—why you care about animal suffering. And if you join with others in your effort, your collective voice will be much stronger than one voice speaking out alone. Many influential animal rights groups started small but ended up making a big difference.

Almost all the "success stories" in this book were due to the efforts of groups of people who used the power of their numbers to drive an issue home. And successes are multiplying as the animal rights movement swells, drawing more and more people at every level of involvement.

If you want to get involved, there's a broad-based animal rights movement you can join, with people working on a wide spectrum of activities—from writing letters to organizing anti-fur campaigns to demonstrating at research labs. Whatever issues interest you most, you can surely find a group that will appreciate your talents and energies.

The best way to start is to decide which aspect of animal rights you feel most strongly about. Whether it's wildlife preservation, factory farming, animal research, or endangered species, there's a group working in your area of interest. And if there isn't, you can start one. Once you educate yourself about the issues, you can speak out for animals to your community and to the world.

If we take our belief in animal rights a step further than our hearts and homes, it will speed the day when animals are safe from human cruelty and exploitation.

A LITTLE HISTORY

In the beginning, we humans depended on other animals for our very survival. Sometimes we competed with them for food and shelter. At other times we hunted other animals for food, or were ourselves hunted. But whether hunters, herdsmen, or farmers, we depended for our sustenance on the animals we killed, the flocks we tended, or the draft animals that pulled our plows.

Early cave drawings clearly depict the intimacy of day-to-day relationships between human and nonhuman animals. One common theme that recurs in surviving folk tales, songs, dances, and legends from around the world is the dilemma of how humans should treat fellow animals. In many hunting cultures dependent on animals for food and raw materials, the hunter was obliged to thank the animal's spirit for allowing itself to be killed.

This intimacy fostered a deep sense of empathy and an appreciation of shared struggle and labor. The advance of technology reduced this basic dependence on animals in all but a small number of cultures and stripped away the daily contact that had long nurtured respect between humans and nonhumans.

Both the Hindu and Buddhist religions express compassion for animals. In the West, the fundamental uniqueness of humans—and inferiority of animals—was established in biblical passages that assert man's dominion over "every living thing." Aristotle formalized the distance between humans and other animals by proposing a "scale of nature" that placed all beings on a ladder from highest to lowest in form. God occupied the top rung, followed by angels, humans, and down through the animals. Humans were further ranked by sex and race with white males occupying the pinnacle. This rigid hierarchy was viewed as fixed and permanent.

In the 1600s, René Descartes, the father of modern philosophy, championed rational man by declaring "I think, therefore I am." Because animals didn't appear to think, Descartes relegated their nature and behavior to a category of machines. Animals were seen as mere automatons, incapable of pain, suffering, pleasure, or thought. Humans were absolved of any moral obligation toward them—a convenient philosophy at a time when people studied anatomy by vivisection, the cutting open of live animals.

There were some notable exceptions to this view. Francis of Assisi, who is as well known for his love of animals and nature as for his fellow humans, referred to animals as his brothers and sisters. In recognition of his kindness and love, many churches have a blessing of the animals commemorating the Feast of St. Francis each October.

A handful of other thinkers, including John Locke, Jeremy Bentham, and Thomas Paine, displayed a courageous concern for the treatment of animals during the 1700s. Bentham rebelled against prevailing opinion by declaring, "The question is not, Can they reason? nor, Can they talk? but, *Can they suffer?*" His insight endures as a moral guide for today's animal rights movement.

The emerging science of biology lent new weight to these moral arguments. Ironically, a century of cruel vivisection had demonstrated that the nervous system of a cat or dog was quite similar to our own. It seemed that animals could indeed feel pain, after all. The Swedish botanist Carolus Linnaeus included humans alongside other mammals in his ground-breaking work, *Systema Naturae*, in

1735. In the late 1800s, Charles Darwin put all species on a continuum of life and argued that certain abilities and characteristics evolve from a primitive into a more complex form. Therefore, "lower" animals have many of the traits of "higher" animals, such as the ability to feel pain or to think. Darwin's writings helped to sweep away arbitrary distinctions between human and nonhuman animals.

Widespread exploitation of children and workers in the 1800s pointed up a clear need to protect people from abuse. Legal protection for animals followed. One English milestone was the Martin Act of 1822, which prohibited the cruel treatment of cattle. In 1824, the Society for the Prevention of Cruelty to Animals was founded (SPCA). The "social correctness" of protecting animals from cruelty was assured in 1840 when the SPCA received royal patronage and became the Royal SPCA.

The animal protection movement crossed the Atlantic in 1866 when Henry Bergh founded The American Society for the Prevention of Cruelty to Animals (ASPCA). Regional SPCAs rapidly flourished across the country. The growth of the humane movement clearly reflected a new spirit of the times.

These early animal protectionists faced a daunting challenge. Abuse of animals *and* humans was widespread in nineteenth-century America—slaves toiled in the fields, children worked 12-hour days in factories (Henry Bergh also founded the Society for Prevention of Cruelty to Children), and horses died pulling overloaded carts in city streets. The SPCAs worked tenaciously to pass and enforce new laws that would afford animals some degree of protection from cruel treatment.

These forerunners of the modern animal rights movement anticipated most of today's central issues. They wrote and spoke out against the cruelties of hunting, livestock raising, vivisection, and the abusive use of animals in work and entertainment.

A new concern for wildlife and nature was born with the

conservation movement in the early twentieth century. Our first national parks and wilderness areas, preserves where wildlife would be safe within their natural habitats, were established at this time. This appreciation of intact natural communities foreshadowed today's concern with endangered species and the interdependence of all life.

After its initial rapid growth, the humane movement waned during the social upheaval of the early 1900s and two world wars. It reemerged in the 1950s with the founding of the Animal Welfare Institute and the Humane Society of the United States.

The publication of Peter Singer's *Animal Liberation* in 1975 signaled the birth of today's animal rights advocacy. Singer documented many of the instances of suffering by over 5 billion animals a year in the United States alone, including factory-farm animals and animals used in laboratory tests. And he reinvigorated the animal protection movement with a well-reasoned and updated philosophy. He argued that human domination of other animals constitutes "speciesism," an unjustified oppression that should be abolished along with racism and sexism.

Just as the early growth of animal protection in the 1800s was allied with advocacy for women, children, workers, and slaves, the contemporary animal rights movement followed in the wake of activism for civil rights, women's rights, and environmental issues. Animal advocates have adopted protests, civil disobedience, and consumer boycotts as new and important strategies.

An impressive string of successes has proved the effectiveness of these nonviolent tactics in expanding animal protection. In 1977, after just a year and a half, Henry Spira's campaign of leafletting and public education succeeded in halting cruel experiments on cats at the American Museum of Natural History. Alex Pacheco's exposure in 1981 of painful experiments on monkeys in a Silver Spring, Maryland, laboratory drew national attention to the extreme suffering that can take place in the name of scientific research. Pro-animal themes are now starting to show up in TV news and on sitcoms. Polls show that a majority of the public supports the spaying and neutering of companion animals, a ban on leg-hold trapping, and an end to cruel product testing.

Vegetarianism is viewed as a healthful, positive alternative to meat-eating. In 1990, a consumer boycott of tuna succeeded in clearing American supermarket shelves of tuna caught along with dolphins. Fur sales are declining as fur becomes widely recognized as a symbol of animal suffering rather than social status. Perhaps most telling is the fact that newspapers no longer use quotation marks when discussing animal rights.

Today, over 10 million Americans from all walks of life belong to organizations advocating the protection and rights of animals. Animal rights is no longer a fringe cause. Its underlying principle of leading a compassionate lifestyle is slowly but surely becoming part of mainstream culture and thinking. More and more people are coming to recognize that we must live non-exploitatively alongside other species—in harmony with nature, not in selfish domination of it.

HOW TO GET INVOLVED IN ANIMAL RIGHTS

Read a book

This book may have been a starting point for learning about ways you can reduce animal suffering. But for every chapter in this book, there are numerous other books that can teach you more about those issues. If this book has sparked your interest, we hope you'll take the time to read some more, to educate yourself and the people around you.

Some of the best books to start with are Peter Singer's *Animal Liberation, Returning to Eden* by Michael Fox, and *The Animal Rights Controversy* by Laurence Pringle. If you're new to vegetarianism, you should take a bite of *Diet for a New America* by John Robbins. We've listed several other books in Chapter Eight that are recommended reading for anyone interested in animal rights.

Write a letter

According to the House of Representatives postmaster, animal rights ranks with catastrophic health care, Social Security policy, and gun control in generating mail to Congress. All those letters (and votes!) have an impact on legislators, who are concerned about keeping their constituents happy.

Writing letters to everyone from newspapers to company executives can be a very effective way of educating others about animal rights. But it's important that your letters be factual, straightforward, and courteous. No one's going to respond favorably to an accusatory, threatening, or scrawled letter.

➤ Always sign your name and give your address. Anonymous letters lack the conviction of signed ones.

➤ Letters to legislators should be concise and to the point. Ask the legislator to support a particular animal rights bill or to vote against a bill that is harmful to animals. Provide some well-researched information about the issue, state your concern, and leave it at that. Letters over a page long often don't get read.

Address members of the U.S. Congress as follows:

The Honorable (first and last name)
U.S. Senate (or House of Representatives)
Washington, DC 20510 (20515 for the House)

➤ Letters to the editor of newspapers should also be brief and well reasoned. Write in response to articles written about animals, or add an animal perspective to an issue the newspaper covered without mentioning animals. Letters should be typed, double-spaced, and usually not exceed about 300 words. Put interesting tidbits of information in the letter that readers might not know.

➤ If a television station airs a program with an animal rights angle, call or write them, too, to let them know how you feel.

➤ Letters to company executives can be effective, especially when tens or thousands of people write in to protest anti-animal practices. Be polite when you write, explaining to a company that you won't buy their products until they stop exploiting animals. If a company has a toll-free product or service number, call that number to complain about their cruel treatment of animals.

Take a class in animal rights

One way to get started in the animal rights movement is to take an introductory class on the topic. People for the Ethical Treatment of Animals (PETA) conducts seminars all over the country for people who are interested in becoming more active in animal rights. The seminars teach people how to shop for cruelty-free products, how to work with the media, how to investigate animal abuse, and how to organize animal rights groups, actions, and demonstrations. Call PETA's Action Line at 301-770-8980 for information. If you can't take the class, PETA has a booklet on becoming an animal activist that will help you to get started.

Annual conferences conducted by the Humane Society of the United States (HSUS), the American Humane Association, and the National Alliance for Animal Legislation also provide good opportunities to become better acquainted with animal rights issues.

Investigate and report animal abuse

What should you do if you come across a situation where you see animal mistreatment or abuse? You're walking through a pet store, for example, and you find that the animals there are kept in dirty cages, appear sick, or are crowded together. Or maybe you have a neighbor who chains his dog up in the heat of day or keeps exotic or wild animals caged in his backyard.

It may be that a simple phone call to a local humane society, animal protection group, or city animal office will take care of the problem.

If not, you can still do something about animal abuse. You can conduct your own investigation. Start by getting a notebook and documenting the instances of cruelty you witness. Detail when, where, and how the incidents happened. Be sure to get names of the people responsible and describe the animals involved. If you make phone calls, take notes on them as well. Photographs or videotape of the abuse will help you bring some sort of action against the animal abuser.

The Animal Legal Defense Fund has put out an excellent booklet, *The Animals' Advocate: Investigating Animal Abuse*, which will help you in your investigation. Written by attorneys for use by laypeople, the booklet describes federal statutes and state laws governing the care and treatment of animals. It also gives tips on documenting cruelty, working with legislators, attorneys, and the media, and using the Freedom of Information Act. The booklet is available for $2.50 from ALDF, Box 4066, Rockville, MD 20850.

Join a group

Joining an animal rights group is a great way to educate yourself about an issue and to get involved with positive action. Your financial contributions to animal advocacy groups will also help support lobbying efforts for pro-animal legislation and public education about animal rights.

But shop around before you join a group. Ask yourself what issues you are most passionate about. It may be that you have an affinity for a certain type of animal that you want to see protected. Whether it's deer, dolphins, wolves, whales, primates, prairie dogs, or songbirds, there's apt to be a group you can join that works to help that animal. Or you may be especially interested in issues that support and reflect changes in your lifestyle, such as vegetarianism, veganism, or being a compassionate consumer. You may be angry about animal research and vivisection, you may be frightened for the future of our wildlife, or you may be interested in learning as much as you can about a variety of animal issues in a broad-based organization. Join a group whose goals and tactics you're comfortable with.

In Chapter Eight you'll find a list of animal rights organizations grouped by interest area. Write to the ones that interest you, and see what issues and actions they focus on. For more information about different groups' activities, you might also want to subscribe to one of the animal rights magazines listed in Chapter Eight.

A coalition of animal protection organizations has drafted an animal rights agenda for the 1990s. This document sets out distinct goals and guidelines for promoting animal protection in laboratories, on farms, in the wild, and in local communities. You can get a free copy of these Joint Resolutions by writing to The American Society for the Prevention of Cruelty to Animals (ASPCA), the Humane Society of the United States (HSUS), or the Massachusetts SPCA.

Start your own group

Along with national groups, dozens of local organizations have had a significant impact on animal rights. Grassroots action is particularly effective in attacking animal abuse on a local level. If there is no animal rights group in your community, or no organization that is working on the specific issue you care about, you might want to start your own group. There are a few things you should consider before you start printing up your letterhead, though.

Gauge your commitment to activism. You need to clarify how much time you can devote to starting a new group. If you're not sure you can handle a full-fledged organization, you might want to incorporate animal rights programs into groups that already exist in your community—your school, church, political group, women's group, men's group, reading group, or community center. You could put on an animal rights program, showing a videotape and leading a discussion afterward. You can get videotapes from national animal rights organizations such as PETA, the ASPCA, the HSUS, and others listed in the next chapter.

Decide what issues to focus on. Animal mistreatment is so widespread that it's impossible to cover all areas of abuse. Focus on one that affects animals in your community. For example, if there is proposed commercial development of a piece of land that local animals depend on for habitat, you could organize to preserve it as a wildlife refuge. Or if a nearby lab or school experiments on animals, you can try to open that institution's practices to citizen oversight.

Read your local papers closely for stories about treatment of animals. Check out local shelters, zoos, boarding kennels, and laboratories to find out how the animals are treated. If there are other animal rights or environmental groups in your area, find out what issues they're working on.

Educate yourself about your chosen issues. Read everything you can get your hands on. Study the laws that relate to the issues, and learn the opposition's arguments. Unless you're well-informed and reasoned, you're not going to convince anyone of your point of view.

Get to know other local and national groups that do animal rights work related to your issue. You'll want to have their names and numbers handy for referrals or quick information when you need it. Set up a filing system for news clippings and other reference materials.

Keep careful track of financial records, meeting notes, and fliers. Once you get started, you'll also want to take care of other important logistical details: a bank account, P.O. mailing address, stationery, business phone, and business cards. You want to look professional from the start.

Create a list of local and national media contacts—and keep it updated.

Find a place for your group to meet (a church, organization meeting rooms, or an office after hours), and prepare an agenda. Set goals. Pool information and skills. Share leadership responsibilities and try to operate by consensus whenever possible. Decide on one or more projects, then develop a timetable and plan of action.

The easiest project to begin with may be a campaign initiated by a national animal rights group. That way you'll already have information and outlines to work from. Or you might want to start a local campaign, creating educational materials for table displays at shopping streets and malls. Other effective tactics include leafletting and letter-writing campaigns. You might want to stage a protest or demonstration on a particular issue—picketing a fur store or an animal research lab, for example. It always helps to be well organized when you conduct a public demonstration. Anything you can do to attract a little more attention without detracting from the issues—such as making banners, dressing in costumes, or performing street theater—is a big help.

For more information on starting a group, write to PETA at P.O. Box 42516, Washington, DC 20015-0516, or call the PETA Action Line at 301-770-8980.

KEEP SPEAKING OUT FOR ANIMALS

The humane movement has made great strides in protecting animals from cruelty and abuse. But animal exploitation is so widespread in our society that there is always plenty of work for compassionate people who want to get involved. We hope you'll play an active role in the ongoing fight for animal rights.

We'd like to leave you with the following declaration on animal rights that was proclaimed and adopted by the 30,000 participants in the March for the Animals in Washington, D.C., on June 10, 1990.

Declaration of
the Rights of Animals

Whereas it is self-evident

That we share the earth with other creatures, great and small

That many of these animals experience pleasure and pain

That these animals deserve our just treatment and

That these animals are unable to speak for themselves

We do therefore declare
that these animals

Have the right to live free from human exploitation, whether in the name of science or sport, exhibition or service, food or fashion

Have the right to live in harmony with their nature rather than according to human desires

Have the right to live on a healthy planet

chapter eight

WHO, WHAT, WHERE: AN ANIMAL RIGHTS DIRECTORY

WHO, WHAT, WHERE: AN ANIMAL RIGHTS DIRECTORY

Once you've read this book and become aware of the many problems and injustices animals face, you may want to pursue your interest in animal rights. Below, we've listed some books, publications, and groups from the animal rights movement. We also list addresses for mail-order companies that make compassionate products, as well as other resources for animal activists. This list isn't comprehensive, so if we've left anyone out, that doesn't mean we don't think they're doing important work. Write to us at Living Planet Press, Box W, 558 Rose Ave., Venice, CA 90291, and tell us about new books, groups, or resources. We'll spread the word.

RECOMMENDED READING

Books

Animal Liberation. Peter Singer. Random House, revised 1990. This is the book that really got the animal rights movement rolling in the '70s; it presents the philosophical underpinnings of our concern for animals.

The Case for Animal Rights. Tom Regan. University of California Press, 1983. Nominated for a Pulitzer Prize, this book tackles major philosophical issues about animal rights.

In Defense of Animals. Peter Singer, ed. Harper & Row, 1985. Essays by prominent animal rights activists on topics ranging from laboratory testing to factory farming to zoos and endangered species.

Animal Rights and Human Obligations. Tom Regan and Peter Singer, eds. Prentice-Hall, 1976. An anthology of scholarly essays on animals by Darwin, Thomas Aquinas, Voltaire, and others.

Of Mice, Models, and Men: A Critical Evaluation of Animal Research. Andrew N. Rowan. State University of New York, 1984. A comprehensive look at the use of animals in research, presenting scientific information in an accessible manner.

Animal Factories. Jim Mason and Peter Singer. Crown, 1980. A documentation, with photos, of conditions on factory farms.

The Animal Rights Controversy. Laurence Pringle. Harcourt Brace Jovanovich, 1989. An even-handed overview of the controversy between animal activists and the research and farming industries.

Returning to Eden. Michael Fox. Viking, 1980. A scathing and eloquent indictment of humankind's cruel exploitation of animals.

Diet for a New America. John Robbins. Stillpoint Publishing, 1987. This "bible" for vegetarians describes how eating meat not only causes animal suffering, but human and ecological problems as well.

The Animal Shelter. Patricia Curtis. Lodestar Books, 1984. A history of the animal welfare movement, as well as an inside view of an animal shelter.

The Extended Circle: A Dictionary of Humane Thought. Jon Wynne-Tyson, ed. Centaur Press Ltd., 1985. An anthology of humane quotations throughout history.

Man Kind? Cleveland Amory. Harper & Row, 1974. An in-depth look at humans' treatment of nonhuman animals.

The Dreaded Comparison. Marjorie Spiegel. New Society

Publishers, 1988. This book draws parallels between human and animal slavery.

The Plague Dogs. Richard Adams. Fawcett Crest, 1977. A warm story about two dogs who are fugitives from an animal research laboratory.

Publications

Animals Magazine, 350 Huntington Ave., Boston, MA 02130

The Animals' Agenda, P.O. Box 6809, Syracuse, NY 13217

The Animals' Voice, P.O. Box 341-347, Los Angeles, CA 90034, 213-204-2323

Between the Species, P.O. Box 254, Berkeley, CA 94701

ANIMAL RIGHTS GROUPS

Multi-issue groups

These groups work on many animal rights issues and distribute a variety of publications and materials.

Alliance for Animals, P.O. Box 909, Boston, MA 02103

American Humane Association, 9725 East Hampden Ave., Denver, CO 80231

The American Society for the Prevention of Cruelty to Animals (ASPCA), 441 East 92nd St., New York, NY 10128

Animal Allies, P.O. Box 35063, Los Angeles, CA 90035

Animal Liberation Network, P.O. Box 983, Hunt Valley, MD 21030

Animal Protection Institute of America, P.O. Box 22505, Sacramento, CA 95822

Animal Rights Mobilization, P.O. Box 1553, Williamsport, PA 17703

Animal Welfare Institute, P.O. Box 3650, Washington, DC 20007

Coalition to End Animal Suffering and Exploitation (CEASE), P.O. Box 27, Cambridge, MA 02238

Focus on Animals, P.O. Box 150, Trumbull, CT 06611

Friends of Animals, P.O. Box 1244, Norwalk, CT 06856

The Fund for Animals, 200 West 57th St., New York, NY 10019

Humane Society of the United States, 2100 L St., NW, Washington, DC 20037

People for the Ethical Treatment of Animals (PETA), P.O. Box 42516, Washington, DC 20015-0516

World Society for the Protection of Animals, 29 Perkins St., P.O. Box 190, Boston, MA 02130

Companion animals

These groups mainly work on companion animal issues, but many work on more broad-based animal rights issues.

The Anti-Cruelty Society, 157 West Grand Ave., Chicago, IL 60610

Massachusetts Society for the Prevention of Cruelty to Animals (MSPCA), 350 South Huntington Avenue, Boston, MA 02130

Progressive Animal Welfare Society (PAWS), 15305 44th Ave. W, P.O. Box 1037, Lynnwood, WA 98046

San Francisco Society for the Prevention of Cruelty to Animals (SFSPCA), 2500 16th St., San Francisco, CA 94103

Sports and entertainment

Committee to Abolish Sport Hunting, P.O. Box 43, White Plains, NY 10605

Performing Animal Welfare Society, 11435 Simmerhorn Rd., Galt, CA 95632

Farm animals

Food Animal Concerns Trust, P.O. Box 14599, Chicago, IL 60614

Farm Animal Reform Movement, 10101 Ashburton Lane, Bethesda, MD 20817

Humane Farming Association, 1550 California St., Suite 6, San Francisco, CA 94109

United Animal Defenders, Inc., P.O. Box 33086, Cleveland, OH 44133

Laboratory animal protection

Alternatives to Animals, P.O. Box 7177, San Jose, CA 95150

American Anti-Vivisection Society, 801 Old York Rd., Suite 204, Jenkintown, PA 19046

In Defense of Animals, 21 Tamal Vista Blvd., #140, Corte Madera, CA 94925

Last Chance for Animals, 18653 Venture Blvd., #356, Tarzana, CA 91356

National Anti-Vivisection Society, 53 West Jackson Blvd., Suite 1550, Chicago, IL 60604

New England Anti-Vivisection Society, 333 Washington St., Boston, MA 02135

Professional organizations

Animal Legal Defense Fund (ALDF), 1363 Lincoln Ave., San Rafael, CA 94901

Association of Veterinarians for Animal Rights, 15 Dutch St., Suite 500-A, New York City, NY 10038

National Association of Nurses Against Vivisection, P.O. Box 42110, Washington, DC 20015

Physicians Committee for Responsible Medicine, P.O. Box 6322, Washington, DC 20015

Psychologists for the Ethical Treatment of Animals, P.O. Box 87, New Gloucester, ME 04260

Scientists Center for Animal Welfare, 4805 St. Elmo Ave., Bethesda, MD 20814

Scientists Group for Reform of Animal Experimentation, 147-01 3rd Ave., Whitestone, NY 11357

Legislative organizations

Committee for Humane Legislation, 30 Haviland, South Norwalk, CT 06856

The National Alliance for Animal Legislation, P.O. Box 75116, Washington, DC 20013-5116

United Action for Animals, 205 East 42nd St., New York, NY 10017

Marine life preservation groups

American Cetacean Society, P.O. Box 2639, San Pedro, CA 90731

Center for Marine Conservation, 1725 DeSales St., NW, Washington, DC 20036

Greenpeace, P.O. Box 3720, 1436 U St., NW, Washington, DC 20007

Marine Mammal Fund, Fort Mason Center, Bldg. E, San Francisco, CA 94123

Wildlife groups

Defenders of Wildlife, 1244 19th St., NW, Washington, DC 20036

Earth Island Institute, 300 Broadway, Suite 28, San Francisco, CA 94133

International Fund for Animal Welfare, P.O. Box 193, Yarmouth Port, MA 02675

Rainforest Action Network, 301 Broadway, Suite A, San Francisco, CA 94133

Wildlife Information Center, Inc., 629 Green St., Allentown, PA 18102

Groups for specific animals

American Horse Protection Association, 1000 29th St., NW, Suite T100, Washington, DC 20007

Bat Conservation International, P.O. Box 162603, Austin, TX 78716

The Beaver Defenders, Unexpected Wildlife Refuge, Inc., Newfield, NJ 08344

Friends of the Sea Otter, P.O. Box 221220, Carmel, CA 93922

Greyhound Friends, 167 Saddle Hill Rd., Hopkinton, MA 01748

International Primate Protection League, P.O. Box 766, Summerville, SC 29484

Mountain Lion Preservation Foundation, P.O. Box 1896, Sacramento, CA 95809

Primarily Primates, P.O. Box 15306, San Antonio, TX 78212

Save the Manatee Club, 500 N. Maitland Ave., Suite 210, Maitland, FL 32751

Religious and special interest groups

Feminists for Animal Rights, P.O. Box 10017, North Berkeley Station, Berkeley, CA 94709

International Network for Religion and Animals, P.O. Box 1335, North Wales, PA 19454

Jews for Animal Rights, 255 Humphrey St., Marblehead, MA 01945

Student Action Corps for Animals (SACA), P.O. Box 15588, Washington, DC 20003-0588

PERSONAL CARE COMPANIES

Here are the addresses and/or phone numbers of major personal care products corporations. Call or write to find out if they currently test their products on animals. Ask them whether or not they are conducting research into alternatives to animal testing.

Alberto-Culver, 2525 Armitage Ave., Melrose Park, IL 60160, 708-450-3000

Armour-Dial Co., 1-800-528-0849

Avon Products, Inc., 9 West 57th St., New York, NY 10019, 212-546-6015

Beecham Products, P.O. Box 1467, Pittsburgh, PA 15230, 1-800-245-1040

Chanel, Inc., 9 West 57th St., New York, NY 10019

Clairol, Inc., 1-800-223-5800

Colgate-Palmolive Co., 300 Park Ave., New York, NY 10022, 212-310-2000

Coty, 235 East 42nd St., New York, NY 10017

Estee Lauder, Inc., 350 South Service Rd., Melville, NY 11746

Faberge, Inc., 1345 Avenue of the Americas, New York, NY 10105

The Gillette Company, P.O. Box 61, Boston, MA 02199

Helene Curtis Industries, Inc., 4401 W. North Ave., Chicago, IL 60639

Jergens, P.O. Box 145444, Cincinnati, OH 45214

L'Oreal, 222 Terminal Ave., Clark, NJ 07066

Maybelline, 12900 South Crawford Ave., Alsip, IL 60658

Mennen Co., Hanover Ave., Morristown, NJ 07960

Noxell, 11050 York Rd., Hunt Valley, MD 21030

Procter & Gamble, 1 Procter & Gamble Plaza, Cincinnati, OH 45202

Revlon, 767 5th Ave., New York, NY 10022

Wella Corp., 524 Grand Ave., Englewood, NJ 07631

CRUELTY-FREE SHOPPING

Write to these companies for their catalogues of cruelty-free cosmetics, personal care products, and household cleansers.

Amberwood, Route 1, Box 206, Milner, GA 30257, 404-358-2991

Baubiologie Hardware, 207B 16th St., Pacific Grove, CA 94950, 408-372-8626

Baudelaire, Inc., Forest Road, Marlow, NH 03456, 603-352-9234

Beauty Without Cruelty USA, 175 West 12th St., #16G, New York, NY 10011-8275, 212-989-8073

The Body Shop, Hanover Technical Center, 45 Horsehill Rd., Cedar Knolls, NJ 07927-2003, 201-984-9200

Come to Your Senses, 321 Cedar Ave., S. Minneapolis, MN 55454, 612-339-0050

The Compassionate Consumer, P.O. Box 27, Jericho, NY 11753

Cruelty-free Cosmetics Plus, c/o Liz Grayson, 318 East 89th St., New York, NY 10128, 212-860-8832

Ecco-Bella, 6 Provost Sq., #602, Caldwell, NJ 07006, 201-226-5799

Humane Alternative Products, 8 Hutchins St., Concord, NH 03301, 603-224-1361

Internatural, P.O. Box 680, South Sutton, NH 03273

Life Start Healthways Inc., 3644 North Blvd., Raleigh, NC 27604, 919-872-5433

My Brother's Keeper, 211 South 5th St., Richmond, IN 47374, 317-962-5079

Nature Basics, 61 Main St., Lancaster, NH 03584, 603-788-4141

NEWAY, Little Harbor, Marblehead, MA 01945, 617-631-9400

Red Saffron, 3009 16th Ave., South Minneapolis, MN 55407, 612-724-3686

Sunrise Lane, 780 Greenwich St., New York, NY 10014, 212-242-7014

Vegan Street, P.O. Box 5525, Rockville, MD 20855

311